A Legacy of Champions

THE STORY OF THE MEN WHO BUILT UNIVERSITY OF MICHIGAN FOOTBALL

By Joe Falls, Bob Wojnowski, John U. Bacon,
Angelique S. Chengelis and Chris McCosky

Francis J. Fitzgerald, Editor

Published by

CTC
PRODUCTIONS & SPORTS

ACKNOWLEDGEMENTS

Research assistance: Bruce Madej, B.J. Sohn,
Jim Schneider, Tara Preston, Sue Vershum and the
University of Michigan Sports Information Office;
Greg Kinney and the Bentley Library, the University
of Michigan; Bob Rosiek; Alan Whitt, Mike Katz, Jim
Russ, Matt Rennie and The Detroit News archives.

ISBN: 0-9654671-0-4
ISBN: 0-9654671-1-2 (LEATHERBOUND EDITION)

Cover design by Chris Kozlowski & Shayne Bowman
Text design by Shayne Bowman
Typeface: Kis-Janson

PUBLISHED BY:
CTC Productions & Sports
37400 Hills Tech Drive
Suite 200
Farmington Hills, MI 48331
(810) 848-1100

"Those who stay will be champions."

— BO SCHEMBECHLER

CONTENTS

Fielding Yost: The Tradition Maker

Fritz Crisler: Genius on the Gridiron

Bo Schembechler: A Return to Glory

Ten to Remember

INTRODUCTION

By Bob Wojnowski

You see it on the helmet, hear it in the song, smell it in the big old stadium. It's the winged stripe and the high-stepping band and the mingled scents of old cigars and fresh cider. Tradition is a funny thing. You don't know exactly when it starts, or when it ends, but you know it when you see it, feel it, smell it. It's familiarity. It's the same stadium standing on the same spot since 1927. It's the same crowds — 100,000-plus — since 1975. It's the same uniforms and the same helmets and the same 'M' Club banner unfurled in front of the same tunnel. It's the same fight song giving you goose pimples again and again. It's the same press box, the same scoreboard and the same stadium rim, unfettered by corporate sky boxes.

Amid swirling change, tradition is simple sameness, the familiar scent of burning leaves on a fall afternoon, the familiar crowds on State Street, the familiar rush as you enter the stadium and spy those familiar benches rising 92 rows to the sky.

It is the most precious commodity in sports, rarer by the day, more valuable by the year. It can't be packaged and purchased. It can't be faked or fabricated. In a sports world that changes with the next big contract, the next franchise shift, the next firing, the next hiring, tradition endures in isolated pockets, built by memories, bolstered by time.

The Cleveland Browns are gone. The Southwest Conference is history. Tiger Stadium is doomed. The Rose Bowl has gone to the highest bidder.

The strong endure, bound by basic ideals, woven like a quilt, passed from generation to generation. Michigan football is among the last great traditions in modern sport, a link to simpler times, a bridge to more complicated times. Others surface occasionally, then slip back, with nothing to connect the present to the future, partly because there's nothing to connect the present to the past.

Around Ann Arbor and beyond, Bob Ufer's voice evokes as many memories as Ernie Harwell's. Growing up, you knew very early this was something that mattered. It wasn't just for fathers and grandfathers, or for kids and teen-agers. It was a connection, is still a connection, more than the infuriating Lions, more than any other team on any level.

Saturday afternoons are built around the game. Neighbors and relatives visit from all across the

Fielding Yost, surrounded by U-M students, observe a Big Ten golf match between the Wolverines and Illinois.

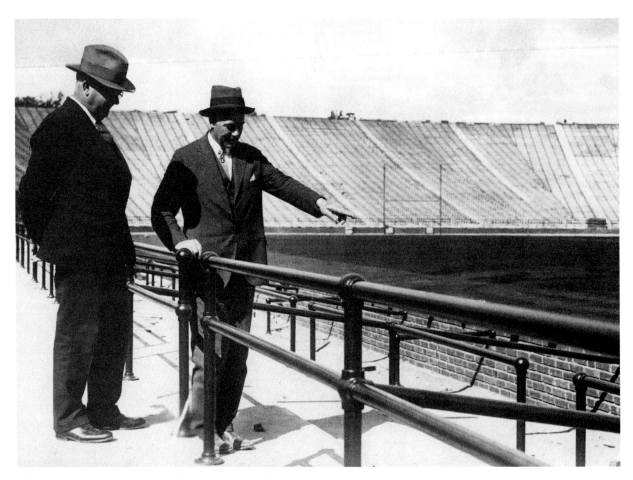

Fielding Yost (right) shows off his new football cathedral to a campus visitor in 1927.

state. For many, Michigan football is 11 annual reunions, and if you don't believe it, walk among the tailgaters at Pioneer High, or try to get into Cottage Inn on a fall Saturday.

Of course, football brings people together across the country, and Michigan doesn't own all the tradition. But no school (save, possibly, Notre Dame) has evoked more passion, among more people, for more years, than Michigan, which mixes all the ingredients. It begins with winning. Winning grabs a basic recounting of history and makes it tradition. It's about winning consistently, to bridge the gaps. It's about winning in familiar fashion — the Celtics' teamwork, the Dean Smith system, the 49ers' offense, the Michigan program.

To install the systems and philosophies that bridge the gaps that generate traditions, you need leaders with vision and strength. You need coaches with a plan, and when you talk about Michigan football, you talk about the coaches and their remarkable plans.

From Fielding Yost, who had the foresight to build a stadium seven decades ago that could be expanded to 100,000-plus, to Fritz Crisler, who invented the two-platoon system and put the famous winged stripes on the helmets, to Bo Schembechler, who uttered the mantra, "The Team! The Team! The Team!" Michigan has harnessed the power of incomparable leaders, men who knew the elements that would endure.

Other schools have had more great players, more Heisman winners. Others have won more national titles — Michigan's last was in 1948. But few have stayed the course as fervently as Michigan, which protects tradition almost zealously. For years, Schembechler railed against the late kickoffs and the portable lights. When the Big Ten recently voted to alter its Rose Bowl contract, another step toward a national playoff, Michigan was the only school to dissent.

Maybe Michigan protects it's tradition stubbornly at times, but there is something tangible to protect. You hear it in the quivering voice of the late Ufer, as he futilely tries to give the final score, moments after Notre Dame's Harry Oliver kicks a 51-yard field goal with four seconds left in the 1980 contest, handing Michigan a crushing defeat. You see it in the eyes of former Michigan assistant Jerry Hanlon, as he sits in a hotel lobby the night before the Ohio State game, trembling with emotion as he reviews the letter he will read to the players the following morning, telling them how many have come before them, and how much it matters. You hear it in the chants of students — "Don't go Bo!" — outside the administration building in 1982, as Schembechler mulls whether to accept an offer from Texas A&M.

Passion does not happen by accident. It comes from passionate people, and in Yost, Crisler and Schembechler — and so many others — Michigan has been led by men driven by more than a job and a paycheck.

There is an arrogance, absolutely. Yost had it, crushing opponents by an aggregate score of 550-0 while going 11-0 in 1901. From 1901 to 1905, Yost won 55 of 57 games, displaying a brashness that angered some, and a vision that startled many.

Crisler had it. When he was coaching at Princeton and Michigan came calling in 1938, he requested a $15,000 salary, exorbitant for the times, and got it. Crisler, like Yost before him and Schembechler after him, demanded discipline and sweated the details. He brought tear-away jerseys from Princeton, and of course, the winged helmets had a practical purpose — so his quarterbacks could more easily pick out receivers downfield.

"I believed in self-discipline. A man should want to make his contribution as part of a unit, a team."

The words came from Crisler but they might as well have come from Yost, or Schembechler. Details and discipline are threads in the quilt, and another D — devotion — is the biggest thread.

Devotion to Michigan developed quickly in coaches, astounding because none of the big three attended U-M. Crisler, as athletic director, gave one-year contracts to his successors, once telling Bump Elliott, "If you do your job, you have a job."

In later years, athletic director Don Canham gave Schembechler one-year handshake deals, banking on Schembechler's loyalty, who banked on the loyalty of players and assistants. Nothing infuriated Schembechler more than the intrusion of agents in the early 1980's, which sapped a player's devotion to the program and destroyed the player in Schembechler's eyes.

Schembechler did not request loyalty. He demanded it. Midway through the 1989 season, Tony Boles was running wild. He'd just rushed for 158 yards against Indiana, sparking Heisman talk. At his Monday luncheon, Schembechler was asked why he didn't campaign for Boles, and the coach exploded.

"That's not my job!" he shouted. "If you like him, you vote for him! But I'm not going to sit up here and tell you how great he is!"

Schembechler knew he had another back, Leroy Hoard, who was just as good; he knew individual awards did not help achieve team goals; and he knew Boles was struggling academically, and Heisman praise could hinder his schoolwork.

Schembechler was forever loyal to those who were loyal to him, and he exacted revenge on those who crossed him. After Illinois fired Gary Moeller, the long-time Michigan assistant returned to Schembechler's staff. A year later, in 1981, the Illini came to Michigan Stadium and seized a 21-7 lead. Then Michigan pounded. And pounded. And pounded. The final score was 70-21 and Schembechler could not deny he'd run up the total and rang up retribution.

To fully appreciate Schembechler's impact, you need to see his former players when they return to Ann Arbor for reunions, to see their eyes well when they talk of the tough little man who used to patrol the practice field whacking players with a yardstick. The respect never wavered because whether you liked Schembechler's straight-ahead style or not, you loved his honesty.

Asked a few years back how he'd like to be remembered, Schembechler was predictably blunt.

"There was no hanky panky," he said. "We went by the book and we played as hard and tough as we could. And that's it."

To many people introduced to Michigan football during that era, that was the appeal — a tight-jawed toughness that set Michigan apart. The Wolverines didn't win a Rose Bowl under Schembechler until his 12th season, but in some ways, that added to the mystique. If they couldn't win the damn thing the Michigan way, it wasn't worth winning.

The Michigan way hasn't changed much over the years, not really. Schembechler, forever loyal, appointed Moeller to succeed him. Moeller, forever loyal, retained much of Schembechler's staff. When Moeller resigned, athletic director Joe Roberson faced the toughest call. He knew change was unavoidable in college athletics. He knew continuity had worked at Michigan for nearly 100 years. He chose to retain Lloyd Carr, bowing to tradition, mindful of the size of the quilt, and all those threads.

Today, in his office, Carr holds up a tattered letter sweater. It was sent to him by the son of the late Don Swan, a Michigan player in the early 1920's who asked that the coach receive it. Carr clutches that tradition, knowing it's a weapon few others have.

"Crisler said it (tradition) can't be bottled and it isn't something you can buy at the corner store, but it's there to sustain you in times of need," Carr says. "One thing I really believe in is the spirit of men like that. Their love for the university, their love for the guys who played the game and their will to win, those are the things that set them apart. I feel a real sense of obligation because I believe in that tradition. I just hope I'm good enough to carry it on."

Oh yes, it can be humbling. Tradition can sustain a person, tradition can strain a person. The weight of more than a century of football can buckle the broadest shoulders. The sports world changes but history doesn't, and neither do expectations. Michigan always has won. Michigan must continue to win. No excuses. No exceptions.

There is something about being the winningest (756 victories in 117 seasons), the biggest (Michigan Stadium's 102,501 capacity now is challenged by Tennessee) and among the oldest. There is an indelible confidence that never wavers, no matter the opponent or the situation.

"I can honestly say, I've never gone on the field at Michigan with anything other than the expectation of winning the game," Carr says. "That's what I think Crisler was talking about when he said you can't buy it. I saw that in Bo — the belief and the commitment that to win, you had to do it as a team. There is no other way."

Michigan has been blessed by the long coaching runs of Yost (40 years as either coach and/or athletic director), Crisler (10 years, plus 27 as athletic director) and Schembechler (21 years). Canham, the athletic director from 1968-88, was just as integral, and made the history-altering decision to hire an unknown from Miami of Ohio named Schembechler.

Every time the Wolverines entered a down period, a future legend stepped in to invigorate it. From 1959-68, Bump Elliott was 51-42-2 and went to one Rose Bowl. Then Schembechler arrived and beat top-ranked Ohio State, 24-12, in 1969. That was the game that connected the present to the

Fritz Crisler and 1938 Michigan captain Fred Janke at fall practice. The Wolverines finished 6-1-1 that season.

past, and returned Michigan to a place at the national table.

It also catapulted the Michigan-Ohio State rivalry to a new level, and nothing pumps tradition like an old-fashioned rivalry. The 1970's were the glory years, as Michigan and Ohio State slugged it out.

Michigan's tradition wasn't built by the 42-0 beatings of Minnesota. It was built by the bloodbaths with the Buckeyes, solemn battles that pitted state against state, family against family, smashmouth against smashmouth. That tradition swelled as much in defeat as it did in triumph. An entire off-season was spent debating the 14-11 loss to Ohio State in 1972, when Michigan couldn't punch it in from the 1. How many TV sets and hearts were broken in 1973, when Michigan and Ohio

State tied, 10-10, but the Big Ten athletic directors voted to send the Buckeyes to Pasadena?

There was drama every season, as Schembechler and Woody Hayes wrestled for supremacy, all the while building college football's best rivalry. From 1969-78, Michigan and OSU went 5-4-1 head-to-head, with Schembechler holding the edge in victories. Simple drama becomes tradition with the right historical mix. Would Michigan's last-play victory over Indiana in 1979 have been so enduring if the great Anthony Carter hadn't been the one to catch the pass? Or if the incomparable Ufer hadn't been the one to make the emotional call?

Hanlon, a Michigan assistant for 23 seasons, saw all those games, heard all the pre-game speeches, and even gave a few of his own. Since his retire-

ment from coaching, he has remained as a fundraiser with the U-M athletic department. The appeal and pull of Michigan football still astounds him.

"Do you know how many kids said they came to Michigan because of the helmet?" Hanlon says. "People laugh, but that's not something to laugh about. That helmet stands for something. It stands for uniqueness. It stands for all the things carried on by Michigan teams over the years. People come to expect certain things. They grow comfortable with it."

No sport attracts and unifies people like college football. Maybe it's because college football programs manage to retain their identities in a world of flux. Maybe it's because players pick their schools for different reasons (not involving money), instead of being assigned to teams like in the NFL draft. Maybe it's as simple as the fight songs and the helmets.

Hanlon reaches into a filing cabinet and pulls out a letter, one of hundreds he has saved. He wrote it to the team before the 1991 game against Notre Dame, in memory of Vaughn Hoekert, a young Michigan fan stricken with cancer. Hoekert's final wish was to see the Michigan-Notre Dame game, but days before, he passed away.

Hanlon's voice quivers again, and for a moment, he is back in the locker room, reading the words to kneeling players: "Some of Vaughn's last thoughts were about Michigan football. We are truly blessed with our health and our talents. If we give any less than our best, it would be a crime to Vaughn Hoekert and to yourselves."

Those emotional pleas only work if grounded in something real, something special. They work at Michigan because they're spoken by people who have been there, and have no plans to leave. No U-M head coach ever has bolted for a job in the pros.

Before his first season as head coach in 1995, Carr leaned heavily on the tradition's sustaining powers. On a Friday night before the opener, he took the team into the cavernous stadium and read

a quote from announcer Keith Jackson about the Michigan tradition. As the sun set, the players milled about, saying nothing, soaking the moment.

Players stood in end zones where Tom Harmon and Desmond Howard stood. They stared at the seats rising to the moonlight. They understood the quilt, and the threads that bind it.

"It's amazing how many people come here to watch us play, how many players have scored touchdowns on that field," tight end Jay Riemersma said. "It's amazing what that place means."

It's amazing what it has meant, to so many people, for so many years. It's amazing how many people know about the unforgettable "Snow Bowl" game against Ohio State in 1950, about the Little Brown Jug, about Charles White's phantom touchdown in the Rose Bowl.

As the years pass, the pressure to change mounts. Soon, the Rose Bowl might not mean as much. There will be a national playoff. There will be a call for sky boxes at Michigan Stadium, for a bigger scoreboard, for luxurious amenities.

The more uncertain the future, the more we long for the past. Everyone, it seems, is trying to build something these days. They're building on quick success and sudden acclaim, instead of on ideals and philosophies. They're building to win now, make money now, without the thread to connect eras and people.

Tradition is a funny thing. You hear it, you feel it, you smell it. Others covet it but can't buy it. Others mimic it but can't create it. Once you have it, you never lose it. It is the most precious commodity in sports, irreplaceable and irreversible. Take a long look at that stadium and those helmets, at the records and the people, then listen to that fight song, and you will see what generations before you saw, what Yost, Crisler and Schembechler saw, before it even existed. Look hard, look around, and try to find anything to match it.

Bo Schembechler led U-M to the top of the college football world – a lofty status once enjoyed by Yost and Crisler.

FIELDING YOST

By John U. Bacon

The Tradition Maker

Yost's ego was almost superhuman, but so was his charm; his ambition was grand, but so was his vision; his stubbornness was remarkable, but so was his ability to change. Yost's most prominent quality, however, had no counter force: his love for Meeshegan, and all it could be.

The late Bennie Oosterbaan, one of Michigan's greatest athletes, loved to tell stories about Fielding Yost. His favorite took place after the dedication game of Michigan's new 85,000-seat stadium in 1927. Michigan played Ohio State, a new rival, and sent the Buckeyes home with a 21-0 loss.

Yost had quit coaching for good the previous season to devote his full attention to his duties as athletic director. In that informal era, after the game, Yost walked back from the stadium to the campus with Oosterbaan, the star of the team. They were both in high spirits from the day's events, but for different reasons.

"Mr. Yost was feeling pretty good," Oosterbaan told Alfred Slote of *The Ann Arbor Observer*.

"We'd won, and the stadium was completely filled. He turned to me and said, 'Bennie, do you know what the best thing about that new stadium is? Eighty-five thousand people paid five dollars

apiece for their seats — and Bennie, they had to leave the seats there!' "

Oosterbaan's brief story includes much of Fielding Yost's legacy: the winning tradition, the landmark stadium and the obvious confidence that comes with those things.

Fielding Yost was Schembechler before Schembechler, Canham before Canham.

Bo coached Michigan for 21 seasons, Yost for 25. Canham served 20 years as athletic director; so did Yost. Bo helped save college football from being over-run by scandals, while Canham showed athletic departments how to operate without bleeding red ink.

What they accomplished is undoubtedly impressive, but they both say they were simply following Yost's lead.

As the Michigan coach, Yost took a renegade sport and made it respectable, even admirable, dur-

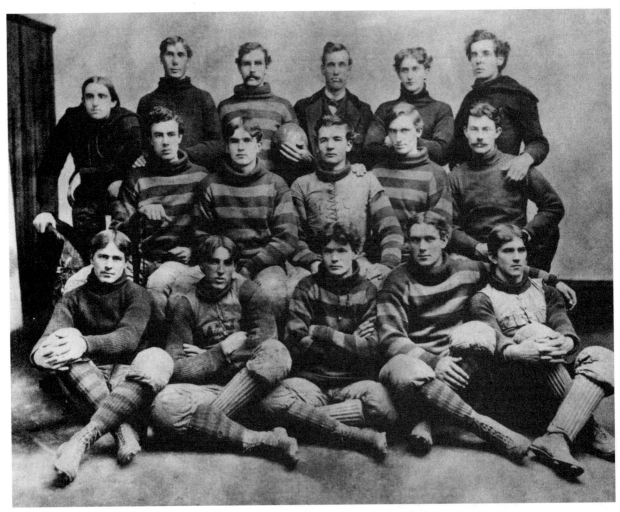

Yost, pictured on the second row, far right, with the 1896 West Virginia football team.

ing its crucial early years. As the athletic director, he transformed the college game from a glorified intramural circuit into a well-run public spectacle, the country's greatest attraction. Perhaps most importantly, he built a foundation for Michigan athletics with such foresight it remains intact today, inspiring countless universities to follow suit.

"We've got the first field house ever built on a campus," Canham says today. "We've got the first intramural building. We've got the largest stadium in the country. That was no accident. That was Fielding Yost."

You could argue Schembechler and Canham are Yost's spiritual offspring. Yost created the model for both, and intentionally or not, most U-M

coaches and athletic directors have shared a surprising number of Yost's qualities.

During practice Yost often put on the pads to show his players how to execute a proper roll-block, then he'd shower, change and go back to his home to charm the socks off the governor an hour later. Like Yost, the Michigan coaches who followed have been both earthy and sophisticated, feeling equally comfortable around football players and U.S. presidents.

After four one-year stints at other colleges, Yost had just turned 30 when he took the Michigan coaching job. Somehow, though, Yost immediately took to "Meeshegan" (which is how he pronounced it, and legendary broadcaster Bob Ufer later mimicked it) and Meeshegan took just as eagerly to

Yost briefly transferred to Lafayette during the 1896 season and played in the team's victory over Penn.

him. The journeyman coach set up roots in Ann Arbor that lasted 45 years. Because of Yost, Michigan has never been afraid to pick a young, well-traveled outsider for the prestigious post of head coach. Crisler and Schembechler readily fit that description, and like Yost, both of them quickly became two of Michigan's most fervent converts.

It all started with Yost.

Though Yost is best known for his "Point-a-Minute" teams, he was hardly a wild, devil-may-care schemer. Quite the contrary, Yost was manic about preparation, tough defense and avoiding fumbles — still hallmarks of Michigan football. Throw in Yost's bent for innovation, and you get 165 wins against only 29 losses and 10 ties at Michigan, for

a winning percentage of .833. Of his 15 seasons coaching in the Big Ten, Yost won the title 10 times. Yost established the sterling reputation of Michigan football, in a sport where success breed success. Bo learned from Woody, Crisler from Stagg — but Yost had to figure it all out for himself.

Yost's standing as one of the all-time great football men would have been as secure as Schembechler's when he stopped coaching in the 1920's, but he went on to double his stature with a 20-year run as athletic director from 1921 to 1941.

In an era when many college presidents thought it unseemly for university teams to draw spectators, let alone charge them admission, Yost tirelessly promoted college football as a public enjoyment, one deserving excellent facilities. Due to his incredible foresight, the buildings Yost created — including the current hockey rink, baseball stadium, golf course, intramural building and, of course, the football stadium — remain some of the biggest and best available, 50 years after his death.

But Yost contributed more to Michigan's tradition than victories and buildings. Yost's powerful personality left an imprint on everybody who met him. He instilled the belief that Michigan's proper place should always be high above the others. The day Yost arrived in Ann Arbor he said, "Michigan isn't going to lose a game" — then backed it up for 56 consecutive contests. Insiders call it confidence; outsiders, cockiness. In the 1970's, when a Michigan State coach called the Wolverines "the arrogant asses from Ann Arbor," he was merely echoing the sentiments of Michigan's foes since 1901.

It all started with Yost.

For better or worse, everything about Yost was larger than life. His ego was as big as the field house that bears his name. When Yost applied for the Michigan job he sent a collection of his clippings and reference letters that weighed 50 pounds — even though Michigan was courting him. But he got away with his excesses because he had the uncanny knack of balancing each vice with an equally strong virtue.

Yost's immodesty may have run counter to society's norms, but he didn't smoke, drink or swear in an era that cherished such restraint. Yost occasionally played up his rural West Virginia background, but this "hay-seed" managed to earn a law degree, run four companies at one time and write

**1896
at West Virginia**

a scholarly 300-page book on football — all on the side.

For such a stubborn man, Yost had some surprising changes of heart. When he arrived at Michigan, Yost didn't worry much about recruiting guidelines, but by the 1920's he had become a stickler for NCAA rule-adherance. In 1907, Yost forced Michigan to leave the Big Ten, but changed his mind 10 years later and became one of the conference's stalwart proponents.

Yost was driven to create his athletic empire, but he also took pains to construct state-of-the-art buildings for non-revenue sports, women and intramural athletes. For years Yost was an undeniable racist who never had a black player on his team, but he later righted himself as the athletic director by demanding a black player be allowed to stay with the team in a Chicago hotel. As usual, Yost got his way.

Yost's ego was almost superhuman, but so was his charm; his ambition was grand, but so was his vision; his stubborness was remarkable, but so was his ability to change.

Yost's most prominent quality, however, had no counter force: his love for Meeshegan, and all it could be. That love drove everything Yost did. A half-century after his death, Yost's love for Michigan still inspires its players and coaches.

It all started with Yost.

The Accidental Athlete

For a man who achieved fame as a football coach and university leader, you'd never guess it from his childhood. Born in the foothills of West Virginia on April 30, 1871, Yost's early life had little to do

Yost's coaching career began at Ohio Wesleyan in 1897 with an impressive 7-1-1 record.

with athletics and even less to do with academics.

The Yost family descends from John Yost, who left Bavaria in 1773 for the Allegheny foothills. Though most of the extended Yost family became farmers, it also produced a surprising number of doctors, one of whom became a pioneer of brain surgery while mending head wounds during the Civil War.

Like many families living near the Mason-Dixon Line, the Yost clan split over the Civil War, with family members fighting for both sides. Yost's dad, Parmenus Wesley Yost, fought for the Confederate Army. Six years after the war ended, his wife, Elzena Jane, gave birth to Fielding Harris Yost, her second of four children.

Yost spent most of his youth working on the 2,000-acre farm that his great, great grandfather purchased near Fairview, W.Va., just 30 miles from the southwest corner of Pennsylvania. As for scholarship, Yost once recalled, "I had not had an opportunity of seeing or reading many books. This was in the country and no books were available."

His mother, a leader of the Fairview Methodist Church, urged him to enroll in the Normal School near their hometown. After a short stint there, he transferred to Ohio Normal in Ada, Ohio, but teaching never grabbed Yost. He didn't like the work, the pay, nor, in all likelihood, the lack of attention the field offered a man of his ego.

These experiences were nonetheless vital to

Yost, second from right, with his 1898 Nebraska squad. The Cornhuskers won the Missouri Valley championship with a 7-3 record.

Yost's developement, because college life brought him under the spell of organized sports. He played first base on the Ohio Normal baseball team and a very crude form of football, which often included a hundred players on a side trying to kick a tattered ball over the opponents' hedges.

Still, Yost couldn't envision making a career as a teacher or an athlete, so he returned to Fairview to help with his father's new general store. Surrounded by an oil boom, his father's shop did brisk business, but his son had larger dreams.

Despite Yost's checkered education, he became a voracious reader, a quick learner and a dogged worker. The combination was enough to gain him admission to the West Virginia law school in 1895. Yost's legal training would prove valuable when he began building the Michigan athletic empire, but not as valuable as his season on the school football team.

Yost was a good looking guy with tossled hair, a broad grin and bright eyes. He was a muscular six feet tall and 200 pounds, which made him one of the biggest players of his generation. (To provide a comparison, as late as 1933, only four of

Michigan's 53 players on its national championship team exceeded 200 pounds.)

As a player, Yost was considered smart, quick and tenacious. He played guard and tackle so well that Park (Dink) Davis, the young Lafayette coach, convinced him to "transfer" midway through the 1896 season to the Pennsylvania school.

Though Yost later claimed he made the switch to try his hand at engineering, as luck would have it his transfer fell on the same week as Lafayette's game against the University of Pennsylvania. Though Penn had a 36-game winning streak, Lafayette upset its highly-touted foe. According to an old friend writing to Yost about those days, Yost returned from the game on crutches with his head bandaged, looking like "a veteran returning from the Western front."

A few days after the Penn triumph, Yost suddenly concluded that engineering didn't suit him after all, and returned to the West Virginia law school a couple weeks after leaving it. When he tried to explain this apparent sleight of hand years later, Yost said he went back to West Virginia because he discov-

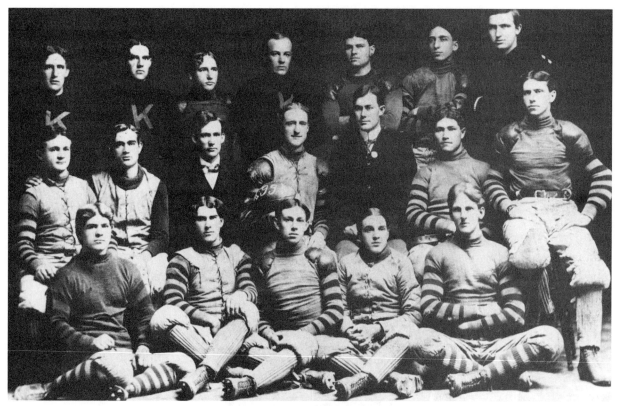

Yost's coaching journey took him to Kansas (top) in 1899 and Stanford (below) in 1900.

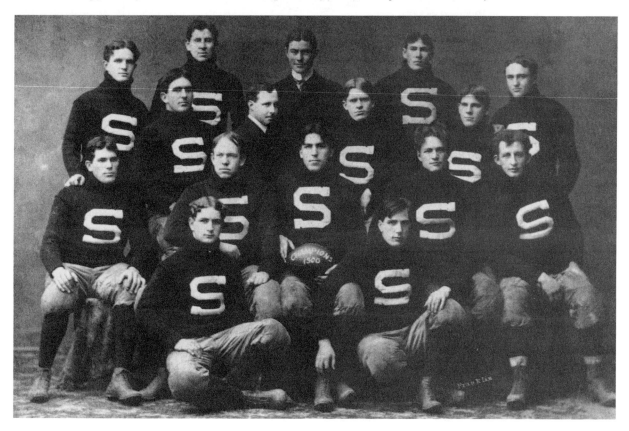

ered engineering involved "too much messing around with figures" — an interesting comment coming from a man who would one day direct two banks and supervise the financing and engineering for Yost Field House, Michigan Stadium and the U-M intramural building. It has to be considered one of the better whoppers of Yost's career.

However, it's worth noting that in the "Wild West" days of college football, such transfers were neither rare nor illegal — and no one would have known that better than Yost himself. Yost studied the rule books of football as copiously as his law school classmates studied their case books.

"In football, as in life," Yost once said, "you've got to know the rules and your rights." But being Yost, he wasn't satisfied with merely being the local expert on the regulations that governed the new game, he had to show off his knowledge to anyone who would listen. Yost's encyclopedic knowledge of the rules would later become one of the hallmarks of his coaching success.

At age 26, with his degree from West Virginia in his pocket, Yost knew that football, not the law, had captured his imagination. "My main objective," he said, "was to see America first, and coaching offered me the best chance to do it."

Of course, Yost had other objectives, too. He was on fire to pile up championships for his teams, and acclaim for himself.

And he was in a hurry to do it.

A Journey to Greatness

Yost made his first coaching stop in 1897 at Ohio Wesleyan, a sister school of Ohio Normal, and wasted no time in racking up a 7-1-1 record.

Though he lost to Oberlin, 14-5, he tied Michigan and beat Ohio State. Those upsets drew lots of attention, exactly what Yost craved. Showing an early flash of self-promotion, Yost declared his players were the "Champions of Ohio" — conveniently ignoring the fact that Oberlin is also located in Ohio.

Despite Yost's early success, he never dreamed of making a career out of coaching — because there were no careers in coaching. In 1897, only Chicago had a full-time coach on its faculty, in part because football teams didn't make enough money back then to cover their expenses. Since no one had the money to keep him, Yost repeated the same routine every year – he took a new job, beat the school's main rival, won the league championship, received glowing reviews, then took his reference letter to get his next job.

The Yost Express made its second stop at Nebraska in 1898. Yost's Cornhuskers beat their arch-rival, Kansas, won the Missouri Valley championship, and finished with a 7-3 record. According to John Behee's biography, *Fielding Yost's Legacy*, the Nebraska people could not have been more pleased with Yost, but, as Nebraska's manager of athletics pointed out, "the financial side of football has never been a success with us."

As proof, Yost received only $160 of the $500 promised him.

"I was on the verge of cutting my coaching career short right there," Yost said, looking back on his career. But as usual, his former employer gave him a glowing letter and he got a new job — working for his former rival Kansas. In 1899, Yost turned right around and beat Nebraska, plus all

**1900
at Stanford**

Legendary college football pioneer Walter Camp visits with Yost prior to the 1903 Michigan-Chicago game.

Yost's 1901 Point-a-Minute team defeated Chicago, 22-0, en route to an 11-0 record.

The 1903 Point-a-Minute team extended their unbeaten streak to 34 games with an 11-0-1 record.

nine other opponents on his way to another championship. He also watched Kansas lose money, then took his latest glowing reference letter to Stanford.

In Palo Alto, Yost set an unofficial record that probably still stands: he won four football championships in one year. Yost notched one title with the Stanford varsity, another with their freshman team, a third with the San Jose Normal school and one more with a Palo Alto high school team.

Stanford loved Yost but had decided at the end of the 1900 season to hire only alumni to coach their teams, a common policy at the time. Still, the four years of job-hopping weren't wasted. The lessons Yost gained would stay him for the rest of his career. Yost's peripatetic background inspired him to schedule teams from far away when few other teams did that, thus enhancing Michigan's profile. He also learned how important rivarlies are to ticket sales and recognition. He never lost to his main rival his first four years, and rarely thereafter. Those results were not accidents. Yost focused intensely on the big games, and often bragged about his record against his rivals. Finally, Yost learned the hard way that no matter how great your talents or efforts, money drives college sports. Without it, you can't keep good people — himself included.

In December of 1900 Yost was out of a job for the fourth time in four years, so he wrote to Illinois to see if they had any openings. They did not, but the manager of athletics there was nice enough to pass Yost's letter on to his counterpart at Michigan, Charles Baird, whom he knew was looking. (Since Yost would go on to beat the Illini six out of eight tries, the Illlinois athletic director probaby rued the day he passed on Yost's letter to Michigan.)

Baird wrote Yost immediately, explaining: "Our people are greatly roused up over the defeats of the past two years," Baird wrote, "and a great effort will be made."

Those were the words Yost longed to hear:

Yost at Whitmore Lake training camp. His personal notes on the back of this photo are below.

25

Willie Heston (fourth from left) and Germany Schultz (far right) led Michigan to a 10-0 record in 1904. The Wolverines outscored their competition, 567-22.

Yost's 1905 Point-a-Minute team's 56-game unbeaten streak came to a halt after a 2-0 loss to Chicago.

Somebody out there was serious about football.

Baird backed up his promise with free room and board for Yost, plus a $2,300 salary — the same money a full professor made — for just three months' work. Against all odds, after years of hustling, Yost had finally found a way to coach football for a living.

Without realizing it, Yost had also found his final home.

If Michigan football is a religion, its converts have been its most fervent believers. Before deciding "this is the place," Yost coached at four schools, Crisler at two, and Schembechler at five. How Yost recognized Ann Arbor was his Valhalla is anyone's guess, but Crisler and Schembechler knew immediately that Michigan was the place for them.

After all, Yost had already been there.

A Meeshegan Man

They didn't call him "Hurry Up" for nothing.

When Yost got off the train in Ann Arbor, legend has it he grabbed his bags and ran up the hill to the campus. Yost had no patience for "rebuilding years." Wherever he coached he expected to win immediately — and he did, every time.

In 1900, the year before Yost arrived, Michigan had a decent year. The Wolverines had a record of 7-2-1 and outscored opponents, 117 to 55, but they also lost to arch-rival Chicago and finished fifth in the Big Ten (which was called the Western Conference then, but referred to here by its current name).

Under their new commander in 1901, the Wolverines won all 11 games, including a 22-0 shocker over Chicago and a 49-0 victory over Stanford, Yost's previous employer, in the first Rose Bowl. The Wolverines scored 550 points that season — an average of 55 per game, which inspired the "Point-a-Minute" title. (Since several games were cut short when the opponent conceded, Yost's team actually averaged more than a point a minute that year — and in the four seasons that followed.)

More impressively, Yost's defense allowed not a single point in return.

Michigan kept up that incredible pace through 1905, racking up 55 wins against just one loss and one tie, outscoring opponents 2,821 to 42. That's right. The average score of a Michigan game during Yost's first five years was 50-1 — and touchdowns were only worth five points back then.

Michigan's victories came in numbers like 119-0, 128-0 and 130-0. Yost offered no mercy, and only an uninformed opponent would have expected any. Yost notched that 130-0 drubbing against West Virginia, his beloved alma mater.

As far as Michigan fans were concerned, Yost's closer victories over Minnesota, Illinois and especially Chicago were far more most satisfying. Yost knew how important it was to defeat a school's main rival; even as Michigan's rivals changed over the years, Yost rarely lost those games.

According to Yost biographer John Behee, "No other coach and no other football team ever so dominated their era as Fielding H. Yost and the Michigan teams for 1901-05." And no other coach ever will. Because of the parity of the modern game, it's highly unlikely the incredible records of Yost's Point-a-Minute squads will ever be eclipsed.

One question: How did he do it?

Winning is in the Details

Like many great football coaches, Yost was a passionate student of military history. (During World War I, Yost charted the troops' movement on a map in his office.) His obsessive game preparation would have impressed any field general. Although the quote has been attributed to a dozen coaches by now, it was Fielding Yost who first said, "Many have the will to win, but few have the will to prepare." That simple phrase has since appeared on hundreds of chalkboards around the country.

To give you some idea of Yost's compulsiveness, in Yost's 1905 football book, *Football for Player and Spectator*, he describes precisely what should be dis-

An end zone view of the first Rose Bowl game on New Year's Day 1902 in Pasadena, Calif.

cussed at training table each night of the week. According to the Yost plan, on Monday night players should turn in their written analyses of mistakes made the previous Saturday; Tuesday should be set aside for a chalk-talk ("The work having been arranged beforehand, only 15 or 20 minutes will be required for the actual blackboard illustrations, leaving the balance of time for singing, talking and joking"); and Wednesday is to be set aside for the weekly "Rule Quiz."

"This should leave nothing unnoticed," Yost wrote, "down to the obscurest section of the laws that govern the game."

He expected all his players to be just as well-versed in the obscurest sections of his own game plan, too. Nothing escaped the coach's attention, and he demanded the same diligence from his play-

ers. He moved the whole team to Whitmore Lake for pre-season conditioning each August and conducted rigorously organized practices, during which he constantly yelled, "Hurry up! Hurry up!" Since most football training in those days was haphazard, conducted by part-time trainers and alumni, Yost's organized, disciplined approach to the game gave his players a huge advantage. While such obsessiveness would probably not be tolerated in the current era of "players' coaches," Yost's boys followed him without reservation.

Kip Taylor remembers Yost well. Taylor played on the 1927 team and scored the first touchdown in the new Michigan Stadium. Though Yost had quit coaching one year earlier to devote himself solely to his job as athletic director, Taylor knew many of Yost's players and the man himself.

Michigan defeated Stanford, 49-0, in this initial contest to complete an 11-0 record.

"The players respected the old man — but not as a close buddy," Taylor explains. "They didn't know him very well. They had him up here," Taylor says, raising his palm above his head, "and they were down there."

Taylor's friend Don Lund, who's been involved in Michigan athletics since he was a three-sport star in the 1940's, added, "Guys did what they were told back then, without questioning it."

But that only explains half of it. Read virtually any document describing Fielding Yost, and you will invariably find the word "enthusiasm" splat-

1902
Rose Bowl game ball

tered all over it. The man was indefatigable, and his enthusiasm was infectious. Ralph Waldo Emerson once said, "Nothing great has every been accomplished without enthusiasm."

Yost had enough enthusiasm to fuel the whole university.

The Hard-Nosed Innovator

Most coaches fall into one of two distinct categories: drill-masters or gamblers. Yost was both.

For being hard-nosed, Yost was Schembechler's equal.

"Fielding Yost is best known for the 'Point-a-

Minute' teams," Schembechler says, "but it's deceiving because he really stressed defense first."

Tell former coaches about the 1901 Michigan team's 550-0 point differential, and they'll be far more impressed by the zero than the 550. You can score 550 points with some good plays surrounded by a bunch of mediocre ones, but to keep the opponent from scoring requires a successful defense on every play of the game, game after game. Just one mistake, and the streak would have been broken. Yost's team didn't set that record with a loose approach to the game.

Schembechler's teams stressed defense first, too, but they didn't always have the size of other teams. In his autobiography, *Bo*, Bo Jackson recalls playing Michigan in the 1984 Sugar Bowl. When he looked across the field at the Wolverine defenders during warmups, Jackson remembered giggling at their relatively small size. But he wasn't giggling by game's end, after taking a pounding all night from a swarm of defenders who "stung like bees." What they lacked in size they more than made up for in technique and hustle.

Fielding Yost predicted the change almost 90 years earlier in his book: "Football is being made more and more a game of physical and mental skill, rather than a contest of mere force." Yost believed speed, smarts and the element of surprise were more important than mere size. He often said, "It takes less effort to fool 'em than it does to knock 'em down."

As the cliche goes, the best defense is a good offense. And the best way to stay on offense is to avoid turnovers. Yost drilled the evil of fumbles into his players as thoroughly as Schembechler did.

Yost wrote, "How many times, by one disastrous fumble, is a team that has apparently won been forced to see its colors trailed in defeat? How many backs, fast, strong and brilliant, have been tried and tried again only to be discarded because of this one fault!" To a Michigan fan, it sounds suspiciously like Schembechler's famous phrase: "No back is worth two fumbles."

**1909
at Michigan**

When Kip Taylor played on the team in 1927, every afternoon at 3 p.m. Yost left his athletic director's office to watch practice and occasionally chip in. "I remember him coming down to practice with his twisted hat — he never had that hat on straight — and cigar juice coming down his chin," Taylor says, providing an oft-repeated description of Yost. "He saw one of us fumble on the goal line, and he stopped practice. We all watched him step over the goal line and back about 20 times. Then he picked up the ball and said, 'Now don'tcha know, you can run over that line all day, but if you don't have this little brown thing (the ball), it doesn't count for anything!' "

As incredible as it may seem, fans back then often accused the architect of the Point-a-Minute teams of boring them with his play calling. Yost always kicked on third down, never on fourth, just to be safe. As a result, his teams often sacrificed first downs for better field position. When the Wolverines went up to play Minnesota one year, both teams were big and tough, and the field was frozen solid, so Yost decided to play cautiously. When the game ended, the Gophers had gained 307 yards rushing and 18 first downs, dwarfing Michigan's 48 yards rushing and two first downs. But Michigan finished with 7 points, Minnesota 6.

Yost studies the architect's building plans for the construction of mammouth Michigan Stadium.

Yost quickly squelched any complaints about play calling with his mantra: "Don'tcha know, it isn't the *first downs* that count. It's the *touchdowns*." If that sounds like Schembechler defending his 3-yards-and-a-cloud-of-dust teams of the 1970's, read on.

Don Canham recalls a story about Michigan's 1923 game against Wisconsin. Fans were very upset about Yost's play calling, with his constant running and third-down punts. After the game a reporter badgered Yost about his conservative strategy, but Yost just turned and pointed at the scoreboard, which said, "Michigan 6, Wisconsin 3."

Yost knew that was all that mattered.

During that same Wisconsin game, the referee missed a Michigan infraction that allowed the Wolverines to score. Badger fans howled at this, but Yost's answer was quick. "Ten years from now, what will the record book show? That [the ref] made a mistake? Naw. I reckon it'll show Meeshe-gan 6, Wisconsin 3."

Still, it would be a big mistake to conclude Yost was conservative. What he was, more than anything, was competitive. If running the ball, avoiding fumbles and punting on third down accomplished victory, that's what Yost would do. But if winning required some razzle-dazzle, Yost was more than willing to do that, too.

Michigan beat arch-rival Chicago, 21-0, in 1902 with lots of daring plays, like a double-lateral that went for a touchdown. Chicago coach Amos Alonzo Stagg patronizingly concluded, "Michigan played a nice game, but it was their tricks that beat us. Their tricks were very clever."

Yost only cared what the scoreboard said, not Stagg.

Yost invented the no-huddle offense in the first Rose Bowl against Stanford, and later came up with the fake kick, both still in use today. He also concocted a potent play called "Old 83," which Michigan teams used successfully into the 1950's. "That play escorted as many touchdowns from inside the 35 as any play ever written," according to Taylor. When the Wolverines were over midfield with 7 or 8 yards to go for the first down, Yost would call "Old 83."

Here's how it worked: the quarterback, the tailback and the left end all started running to the right side, just like an option play — with one important difference: the two ends off the right side jumped in front of their linemates, then cut hard to the left, seemingly in the opposite direction of the play. A split-second before the quarterback committed to the option, however, the tailback reversed direction back to the left, received a pitch from the quarterback, and ran back around the left side. Once the tailback cut the corner, the two guards who'd run to the opposite direction at the outset of the play provided easy passage to the end zone. "The tailback could just walk it in," Taylor says.

"Football is so different now," Don Lund says. "Without the uniforms you couldn't tell who's who. They all have the same formations, run the same plays. But back then it was wide-open. Hey, a tailback had to pass, kick and run back then. There were more possibilities."

Yost naturally took advantage of everything the wide-open style afforded, including the forward pass. In his book he lists six distinct styles of forward passing — one year before it was legalized in 1906. He knew where football was headed. Among the passes he described: the underhand pass, the "end-pass," which looked like a frisbee toss, and the "spiral throw." Yost popularized the now-familiar spiral, and some sources say he invented it.

Notre Dame is often credited with establishing the forward pass as an offensive weapon during the 1912 Army game, a game played in New York City in front of the national media, but Yost actually revolutionized the game two years earlier against Minnesota. Both teams were at the height of their powers in 1910, and neither team could score

against the other's great defense. Finally, in the fourth quarter, Stanfield Wells hit Stan Borleske twice to move the ball from midfield to the Gopher 3, setting up Michigan's only points of the day. Michigan won, 6-0, and kept the Little Brown Jug, but more importantly, somebody had finally found a proper use for the forward pass. That somebody, of course, was Fielding Yost.

"He was a great believer in the forward pass," Kip Taylor says. "But he wanted the passes down the field, coming over the receiver's shoulder. That way the defense couldn't intercept them – and if they did, it was as good as a punt. He said, 'You never risk a turnover for a ham sandwich!'"

Preparation and smarts don't count for much if you don't have the players to carry them out. As Kip Taylor says, "If you're going to build a brick house, you better have bricks. If you're going to build a football team, you'd better have players."

Yost had the players right from the start. In 1901, Yost inherited a number of excellent players from the previous coach, but also added a star from his old San Jose Normal School team.

As Will Perry tells it in his book, *The Wolverines*, Yost wrote to Willie Heston to convince him to come to Ann Arbor, but he declined. Months later, Heston happened to run into a man in San Francisco who'd just traveled from Toledo, Ohio. The man had not used the second half of his round trip train ticket, and sold it to Heston for $25.

Two days after arriving in Ann Arbor, Heston was standing on the corner of Main and Huron streets when someone grabbed him from behind and lifted him off his feet. Surprised, Heston turned to see Fielding Yost.

"Why you little son-of-a-gun!" Yost exclaimed. "You made it, didn't you! I always figured you'd come with me."

Heston was an unusual specimen. He stood 5-8 and weighed 184 pounds, yet he could still beat Olympic gold medalist (and U-M star) Archie Hahn in the 40-yard dash. Heston combined his

Yost instructs a youngster how to drop-kick a football at practice in 1921.

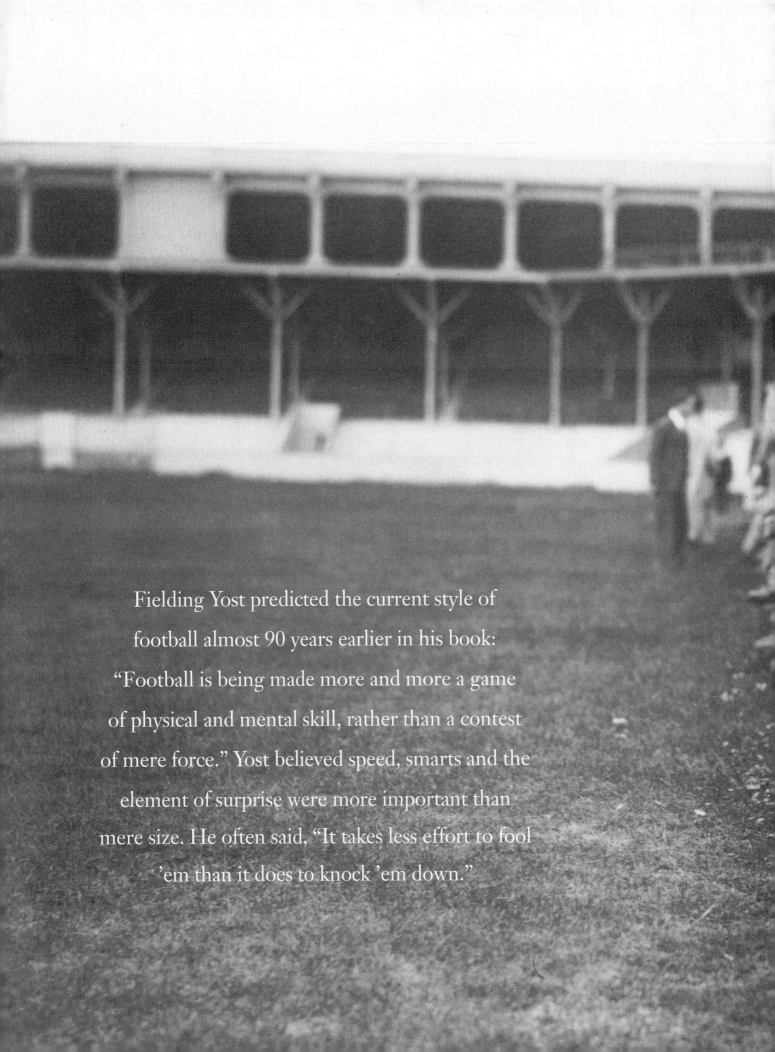

Fielding Yost predicted the current style of
football almost 90 years earlier in his book:
"Football is being made more and more a game
of physical and mental skill, rather than a contest
of mere force." Yost believed speed, smarts and the
element of surprise were more important than
mere size. He often said, "It takes less effort to fool
'em than it does to knock 'em down."

Michigan Gov. Fred W. Green joined Yost to watch the Wolverines' 21-0 win over Ohio State in the 1927 game dedicating Michigan Stadium.

power and speed to run for more than 5,000 yards and 72 touchdowns at Michigan. Yost said, "He was the finest halfback I've ever seen play football."

When Heston left after the 1904 season, Germany Schulz filled his spot. Schulz, a 6-4, 245-pound man from Fort Wayne, Indiana, played center when centers were an integral part of the offense. On defense, he started out as a lineman, but one day in practice he kept dropping back from the line to react to the play better. Yost objected to this until he saw that it worked, then taught it to everyone else.

And that's how the position of linebacker was born.

Schulz had guts. Although his injuries forced him to leave the 1908 Penn game after one half, Yost said, "He gave the greatest one-man exhibition of courage I ever saw on a football field." Schulz did all these things well enough to join Heston on the All-Time all-America team in 1951.

Once Yost brought such dominant players in, rumors inevitably started that he had skirted the rules. It's probably true Yost didn't follow the off-field guidelines on recruiting and the like, but for all the smoke there isn't much evidence of a gun in his files.

Often it was opposing coaches, especially rival Amos Alonzo Stagg, who started the rumors while doing the same things themselves — just not as successfully. Most of the charges were made indiscriminantly, based less on proof of wrong-doing than on a player's ability. Opposing coaches suspected Yost of foul play with both Heston and Schulz, two very different players.

Schulz took a year off in the middle of his four-year playing career — the records don't say why — yet still didn't graduate, on time or otherwise. The suspicions about Yost bending eligibility rules with Schulz were probably accurate.

On the other hand, the same accusations about Heston were absurd. While running as an all-American back on the weekends, Heston graduated from the demanding Michigan law school on time. According to Kip Taylor, "He was no dummy. Heck no. I think the other coaches thought Yost brought in ringers because he brought in good football players — and so they called them ringers."

In any case, the whole question of Yost's early record on ethics needs perspective. As Canham says, "People try to judge Yost in the period in which we're now living, but that was 90 years ago. You have to put it in the proper time frame."

Coaches didn't have many rules to follow back then — they were considered guidelines more than edicts — and there weren't many coaches to follow them, anyway, since most teams were still run by alumni or glorified trainers. The NCAA didn't get started until 1905, and the Big Ten didn't get serious about making rules stick until after that. College football in Yost's early years would be on a par with club sports today.

To give some idea of the informality of the game back then, Michigan scheduled Ann Arbor High School as late as 1891, just 10 years before Yost arrived. (The Wolverines beat the local teenagers, 62-0.) Another example: In 1897, when Yost's Oberlin team played Michigan, Oberlin only had 10 players, so Michigan allowed Yost himself to suit up and play. College football at the turn of the century had a sort of "anything goes" feel to it — not the kind of atmosphere that could expect strict adherence to the rules.

The rules did become more rigid by the 1920's, and to Yost's credit, he changed with the times. But he remained a little embarrassed by the lawlessness of college football in the early 1900's, especially that of his own teams.

College football has produced many innovative, hard-driving coaches with good players. But none of them consistently beat opponents the way Yost's "Point-a-Minute" teams did, before or since. And for a simple reason: none of them probably wanted to beat teams by those scores, except for Yost.

Yost's killer instinct, more than anything else, separated him from the rest.

Living Large

Michigan brought Yost in for a purpose: to win games, win Big Ten titles, and beat Chicago. By 1905, Yost had achieved all that and more. He won 55 of 57 games, four straight Big Ten titles, and four out of five games against Chicago, by a 93-12 margin. (The fifth game, a 2-0 loss, cost Michigan their 56-game unbeaten streak and their fifth straight Big Ten title.)

Given such incredible success, you'd think Yost would have been universally popular. Among students and alumni Yost certainly was, but he was equally unpopular among many faculty members.

For starters, many academicians were suspicious of football itself, since it had been an unruly, unstructured game from its inception. Legend has it that, just a few years after college football began, a group of Michigan players asked the university president for permission to play Cornell in Cleveland. His memorable response: "I will not permit 30 men to travel 200 miles just to agitate a bag of wind."

The faculty also recoiled at the salary Yost received — a football coach! — and was positively galled that he was allowed to skip town 42 weeks a year to tend to his lucrative businesses in West Virginia and Tennessee. (For a few of his annual 10-week stints in Ann Arbor, Yost stayed at the Sigma Chi house.)

Yost didn't help matters with his conspicuously high profile. When Ann Arbor was still a small, walking town of two-story brick buildings where everybody knew everybody, Yost spent his free time going from shop to shop talking about the latest game. His reputation, for better or worse, grew quickly.

Unlike Crisler and Schembechler, for whom the celebrity that came with the job was a benign nuisance, Yost actively sought fame. According to Edwin Pope, the sports editor of The Miami Herald, "When newspapers praised him — they seldom did anything else — he showed the printed applause to everyone within reach, beaming, 'Look 'ere, look 'ere what they say about me.' "

1912
at Michigan

"He'd talk to anyone, and probably talk too much," says Don Canham. "It's why he made great copy. The reporters loved him."

Yost didn't like sharing the podium with other speakers. If someone talked longer than a few minutes, Yost would ask, "How long is this feller goin' to be?" (Yost's inability to share the stage would become a problem in his relationships with Stagg, Knute Rockne and his coaching successors at Michigan.) Yost loved jokes — provided he was the guy telling them. If you wanted to find a camera, all you had to do was put your hand on Yost's shoulder and follow him.

Someone once asked Ring Lardner, the legendary sportswriter, if he ever talked to Fielding Yost. "No," Lardner replied. "My father taught me never to interrupt."

Counter-forces

Since Yost lived in an era in which modesty and moderation were the rule, it's remarkable that people usually excused Yost's extravagant behavior. The reason: for every Yost excess, he had a virtue to offset it.

Yost was undoubtedly egotistical in the extreme, but there was something endearing about his immodesty. Yost was neither self-serious nor vindictive, and his charisma was undeniable. In photographs Yost invariably display a warm, inviting smile, and his voice was rich and gentle — when not yelling, "Hurry up, hurry up!" Lardner, who made a career interviewing the likes of Babe Ruth, Bill Tilden and Knute Rockne, said, "Yost had more personality than any other man I have ever met."

Yost's self-aggrandizement had an innocent, "Look ma, no hands!" quality to it. His ego tended to attract, not repel, like Muhammad Ali's or Reggie Jackson's. Pope, the journalist, wrote that Yost was "an unashamed ham, a natural-born exhibitionist — that rare person who can boast and be liked for it."

If Yost thought highly of himself, he generally thought highly of those around him, too — perhaps concluding that they had greatness by association. Late in Yost's life he bought an expensive birdbath made of Italian marble. When a neighborhood boy etched his own initials on the side of it, Yost summoned him. He took the boy back to the birdbath, pointed to the letters and asked, "Did you do this?" The young boy didn't dare deny it. "Well, do you know what this means?" Yost asked,

Yost, left, watches all-America halfback Harry Kipke perform one of his booming punts.

Yost savors a visit with his 1926 stars Bennie Oosterbaan (left) and Benny Friedman (right).

pointing to the boys' initials. The boy quivered, wide-eyed. Yost then explained, "It means now you're going to have to become a very important man, so I can be proud of this."

Yost promoted the University of Michigan and his team almost as feverishly as himself. He liked to ask, with his cocksure grin, "Who are they that they should beat a Meeshegan team?" He asked the rhetorical question so often, it became the refrain for a popular song. When Yost once asked about Michigan's enduring fight song, "The Victors," he said, "I reckon it's a good thing Louis Elbel was a Meeshegan student when he wrote that song. If he'd been at any other Big Ten school, they wouldn't have had much chance to use it, y'know."

It also helped that Yost and his team looked pretty good compared to the uneducated coaches and brutal brand of football found elsewhere. In 1905 alone, 18 players died on the football fields

around the country and another 159 were seriously injured.

President Theodore Roosevelt himself was a fan of the game, but for that reason he called the coaches and presidents of Harvard, Yale and Princeton to the White House in 1905 to urge reforms. This meeting begat another meeting, which gave birth to the Intercollegiate Athletic Association. Five years later, in 1910, the IAA renamed itself the NCAA, and an institution was born.

Yost himself acknowledged football's problems. "No American game has won so much praise and, at the same time, so much censure, as has football," Yost wrote. "All will concede that the game is rough, but roughness does not constitute brutality. Every player must learn to have perfect control of his temper, so that he may ... never disgrace himself or his school by forgetting what the etiquette of the gridiron demands."

For once, Yost wasn't simply spouting public relations copy. No similar casualties occurred at Michigan, partly due to Yost's emphasis on smart football and sportsmanship over thuggery — not to mention the advanced padding he designed for his players. Though Yost didn't pretend to follow the loose off-field guidelines when he started at Michigan, on the field his teams followed the rules scrupulously. His former employers at Nebraska and Kansas, respectively, wrote that Yost "teaches only straight-forward, legitimate football," and "he insists on clean football." Yost's sense of fair-play on the field set his program apart from many others.

Compared to his coaching peers, Yost stood out as an intelligent, well-educated and well-spoken man — when he wanted to be. Though Yost probably slipped a few players past the eligibility norms, most of his players performed well in the classroom, and did so before grade inflation and the physical education department made things easier for athletes. "He didn't have many dummies on those teams," Kip Taylor says. "Everybody had a goal. They had a plan, and went to Michigan because they loved the university."

Yost's best counter to the many critics of football, however, might be his greatest legacy to the game: In an era when football was considered a social ill run by renegade coaches, Yost argued that, when properly coached, football developed valuable qualities in students that the classroom could not. The belief that football builds character has been repeated so often it is now a cliche, but when Yost first espoused it, it was a fresh idea.

Before sports were adopted on campuses, Yost

**1925
at Michigan**

_____

wrote, students only had two role models to choose from: the bookworm, who was productive, or the card shark, who was admired. Yost believed football resolved this dichotomy by taking the title of "Big Man on Campus" from the hard-living card shark, and giving it to the healthy, hard-working football player. Yost firmly believed football developed the whole person.

"The player must learn to act for himself and quickly," his book states. "His own interests must be subservient to the interests of the team. He must carry his whole heart into every play of the game and must never lose his temper. ... (Given) the severe mental drill given to the player, when he must learn a mass of rules (and) a system of signals and carry them out instantly ... it is very evident that a dullard can never play football properly. ... These same rules, properly carried out, bring success in after life."

We've heard all the arguments a hundred times before — but it started with Yost. The belief didn't stop with him, however, because hundreds of Yost's followers still espouse his faith in the lasting benefits of college football.

President Gerald Ford wrote an article for *Sports Illustrated* in 1974, one month before entering the Oval Office. He recalled his days on the Michigan football team (which won national titles in 1932 and 1933, and named Ford the MVP in 1934), and the lessons he still carried with him.

"If it is a cliche to say athletics build character as well as muscle, then I subscribe to the cliche," he wrote. "The experience of playing the game can be applied to the rest of your life, and drawn from freely."

Now 82, Ford still recalls Yost stressing how

football builds character. "I certainly had the impression that that was the foremost point that Yost always made," Ford says. "If you have character, you can make up for a lot of deficiencies."

Ford took it to heart. According to the official transcripts from his years in the Oval Office, when President Ford interviewed job candidates he invariably asked them if they had played a sport in school, reflecting his belief that those who'd played on a team possessed valuable qualities that others did not.

Schembechler often drew on Yost's philosophy when addressing his team. "This is the Yost quote that we used the most," Schembechler says, then in his typically motivational style he recites Yost's speech from memory.

" 'I ask no man to make a sacrifice. On the contrary. We ask him to do the opposite. To live clean, come clean, think clean. That he stop doing all the things that destroy him physically, mentally and morally, and begin doing all the things that make him *keener*, *finer* and *more competent*.'

"We used this a thousand times," Schembechler says, breaking out of character. "It says it all. You don't *sacrifice* to play football. When we ask you not to drink, smoke or carouse — it's not a *sacrifice*, we're just asking you to be doing what you should be doing *anyway*."

When assessing Yost's reputation in town, it's important to understand what Ann Arbor looked like back then. In the 1840's, Ann Arbor's second decade, both a temperance society and a popular saloon opened up, and the two sides have done battle ever since. Ann Arbor's German immigrants liked their beer, but the city leaders knew Ann

1926
Student caricature

Arbor's main industry depended on its image as a safe place for parents to send their children.

As early as 1863, University of Michigan President Henry Tappan urged residents to "root out the evil influences" of alcohol; a few years after that President Erastus Otis Haven said Ann Arbor was "disgraced all over the country" as a "place of revelry and intoxication." (A century later Ann Arbor mayor Jerry Jernigan would say almost the exact same thing about the city's infamous Hash Bash and $5 pot law.)

The tension between the demands of city drinkers and concern for the young students became so great, over 100 years ago city officials drew a line separating the Michigan campus from downtown Ann Arbor. They allowed alcohol to be served only on the city side of the street, which they called "Division."

Despite the many temptations students faced, Yost could honestly recommend such an ascetic lifestyle for his players because he lived it himself. Journalist Edwin Pope wrote: "(Yost) not only preached against swearing, dirty storytelling, smoking and drinking but sturdily refused to indulge in any of it himself. 'Some people can drink,' he lectured, 'and it doesn't hurt them. But it doesn't do them any good. And ye want to be good, don't ye?' "

Yost's abstinance was very important in a sport sullied by its reputation for revelry, especially in a town struggling to keep students away from city bars. The last thing Ann Arbor needed was a drunken football coach to lead more students astray. Small wonder the new coach's popularity soared among many city and university leaders when a story came out his first week in town. Titled,

A pair of American icons: Will Rogers (left) and Yost in Rogers' last movie, "Old Kentucky."

"Coach Yost Doesn't Touch Liquor," it recounted how some alumni were watching Yost conduct summer practice at Whitmore Lake, and invited him out for a beer afterwards.

"I have never taken a drink in my life," Yost said. "In fact, I cannot even imagine what it would taste like."

"Well, come down and take a cigar, then," one alum suggested.

"Please excuse me," said Yost, "but really I don't like to go into such places."

The temperance society never had a more influential spokesman.

A Team Adrift

From 1906 to 1919, Yost produced a 76-23-8 record. It was a great mark by any standard — except the one Yost had just established. Those 14 years were the most turbulent in Michigan football history.

When the reform-minded Big Ten sought to regulate the game, Yost and his team didn't want to be in the conference any more. Yost was willing to play by new rules governing recruiting, funding and eligibility, but he couldn't stomach the conference's proposals to limit seasons to five games, reduce player eligibility to three years, and insist that coaches be full-time faculty members.

Yost knew if he complied with the new Big Ten regulations, his team would have little chance against schools that weren't held to those rules, especially the Eastern powers. When he arrived in Ann Arbor, Yost was determined to get some respect from the Eastern establishment, and he did. Before the days of polls, writers usually settled informally on one or two teams as the best in

Yost and Ohio State coach Francis Schmidt visit during a change of trains in Chicago in 1935.

the nation. During Yost's Point-a-Minute years, they tabbed Harvard and Michigan in 1901, Princeton and Michigan in 1902, Yale and Michigan in 1903 and Penn and Michigan in 1904. The Eastern representative always changed, but the Wolverines consistently stood at the top of the "West" — and on a par with their Eastern brethren. To sacrifice that hard-won recognition galled Yost.

Adding insult to injury, the driving forces behind these reforms were none other than U-M's own President James Angell and Chicago's Amos Alonzo Stagg.

President Angell simply hoped to return college athletics to the English ideal, which allowed for more student participation and less notoriety for the victors. The idea of strangers with no connection to the university paying to watch them play struck him as odd and possibly dangerous.

Stagg's motives were less altruistic. Though Stagg wasn't any more pious than Yost, he was willing to put up with the changes if it meant slowing down Yost's Point-a-Minute squads. Besides, the University of Chicago had already made Stagg a full-time member of its faculty, an extraordinary move for the time. After losing four consecutive games to the upstart Yost, Stagg had escaped with a 2-0 victory in their last meeting. He probably wasn't anxious for a rematch.

Because Michigan was reluctant to accept all the rules — or perhaps because Stagg was just looking for an excuse — Chicago cancelled its games with Michigan in 1906 and 1907. When it came time for Michigan's Faculty Board in charge of Intercollegiate Athletics to vote, Yost urged them to refuse the conference proposals. They did, forcing Michigan to drop out of the Big Ten in 1907.

That's right: the school most closely associated with Big Ten football at one time left the conference in a huff.

At first the students and alumni were happy with the decision. Yost figured Michigan could still play many Big Ten teams as an independent — much like Notre Dame does today — while leaving room on the schedule to play the best Eastern schools.

It didn't work.

In 1909 the Big Ten passed a rule prohibiting conference teams from scheduling former members who had since withdrawn — an edict clearly aimed at ostracizing Michigan — which they called the "non-intercourse" rule. (The irony was probably unintended.) Consequently, Michigan faced Big Ten competition only twice in their next 107 games — both times against Minnesota — and not once from 1911 through 1916.

Understandably, those contests against Minnesota in 1909 and 1910 took on greater importance because of Michigan's exclusion from Big Ten team's schedules — and also because of a little putty-colored water container. Although most Michigan fans are familiar with the story of the Little Brown Jug, it warrants a brief recap here. In 1903 Michigan tied Minnesota, 6-6, the only time the Wolverines didn't win during Yost's first four seasons at U-M. As the players left the field, they forgot their clay water-jug on the bench. When Michigan wrote Minnesota asking for the jug back, the Gophers replied: You want it, come up here and win it back. Michigan remembered that note when they returned to Minneapolis in 1909.

Adding more fuel to the game, that season Michigan had already beaten Syracuse and Penn, while the Gophers had just clinched the Big Ten title. The Gophers were given the edge, but it didn't matter. Michigan beat Minnesota, 15-6, to reclaim the Little Brown Jug.

Michigan followed it up with a 6-0 victory in Ann Arbor in 1910. Though Michigan's record in Brown Jug games stands at 55-21-3, Minnesota

had the upper hand against the Wolverines in the 1930's and 1960's, and played spoiler twice against highly regarded Schembechler teams. The Little Brown Jug proved so popular, other schools started rivalries around oaken buckets, railroad bells and brass spittoons — but the Jug was first.

Yost's decision to leave the conference had an unintended side effect: By doing so, Michigan switched its main rivals. Michigan didn't play its first arch-rival, Chicago, for 12 seasons, but filled the free date in the schedule by playing Ohio State, not yet in the Big Ten, for the first six of those years. The Michigan State Spartans — then called the Michigan Agricultural College Aggies, but for simplicity referred to here only as Michigan State — appeared on Michigan's schedule for the third time in 1907, but have continued to do so all but four seasons since then.

In hindsight, being dropped by Chicago was a good deal. Michigan lost a rivalry with a school that ended up cutting all sports in 1940 anyway, and gained matches against two opponents who remain Michigan's biggest rivals to this day.

Overall, though, leaving the Big Ten created more problems than it solved. Michigan scheduled yearly games against Cornell, Penn and Syracuse, but Michigan couldn't get the upper hand. Those rivalries were popular both locally and nationally, but to Michigan fans, they never replaced the contests with regional foes like Chicago and Minnesota. Worse, to fill its schedule Michigan had to play teams like Lawrence, Mt. Union and Marietta. And even if Michigan's football team could survive being outcast by the Big Ten, its other varsity teams could not.

The Wolverines were probably also hampered by Yost's off-season endeavors. His investments were savvy and fruitful — one of his stocks jumped from $3,600 in 1908 to almost $20,000 by 1926 — and his work in business produced far more income. At one point Yost served as director of four companies, all located in or near Nashville,

Yost (far right) gathers with fellow 1920's sports celebrities (left to right) Glenn (Pop) Warner, Knute Rockne, Babe Ruth, Christy Walsh and Tad Jones before attending the 1925 Coachmen's Dinner in New York City.

including a major bank, a cement company, a furniture company and the Great Falls Power Company.

This last position required so much work the owner originally wanted Yost only on the condition that he be free 12 months a year. Obviously, with a team to coach Yost could not be available each fall, but he did the job anyway from 1908 to 1914. It's hard to believe the Michigan football team received Yost's full attention during those years. It's a safe bet, however, that Yost's small family didn't take up too much of his time.

Yost met his wife in a circuitous fashion. Yost had been an active member of Sigma Chi when he was in college, and one of his favorite players at Michigan, Dan McGugin, had been a member of the Ann Arbor chapter. In 1904 the two of them attended a Sigma Chi party in Nashville, where the 33 year-old Yost met Eunice Fite, a high society girl in her 20's. They married in 1906, shortly after McGugin married Fite's sister.

Everyone who met them says Yost and his wife made quite a contrast. Eunice was the classic Southern belle, a proper woman who carried herself with poise and distinction. Her famous husband, on the other hand, often wore rumpled pants, his hat on backwards and cigar juice running down his chin (though he rarely smoked them).

Eunice Yost was still alive when Bo Schembechler started coaching at Michigan in 1969. Bo and his wife, the late Millie Schembechler, made a few visits to Mrs. Yost's long-time residence on Stratford, a tree-lined street near the corner of Hill and Geddes, and from these visits the two coaches' wives struck up a friendship. "You could tell from

The Little Brown Jug

the way she dressed and the way she talked, Mrs. Yost was the class of the operation," Bo says today.

It is the plight of football wives, however, to get by with little attention from their husbands. "I wouldn't think the Old Man was the greatest family man in the world," Kip Taylor says. "He loved football and he loved Michigan and that was his whole life. If he could corner you, he'd tell stories by the hour."

Nonetheless, this odd couple established an honest, devoted marriage built on mutual respect. One former neighbor says, "She was a complete support system for him, much like Millie was for Bo. He depended on her, a rock at home."

They had one son, Fielding Jr., who went by "Buck" and played football for Michigan in 1931.

Wolverine Renaissance

In November of 1917, 10 years after Michigan told the Big Ten what to do with its new regulations, both sides agreed it was in everyone's best interest for Michigan to return to the conference. Yost happily submitted to the Big Ten's more temperate rules, and the conference schools welcomed Michigan back without resentment.

Reuniting Michigan with its old Midwestern rivals created a powerful chemical reaction that sizzled immediately, but it also gave off some byproducts that shaped Michigan athletics for decades. At the outset of Michigan's 10-year hiatus from the Big Ten, the Regents replaced "uncooperative" members of the Faculty Board in Control with their own candidates, then further weakened the Board by claiming all Board decisions required final approval from the Regents. The

Yost and U-M coaches (from left to right) Wally Webber, Bennie Oosterbaan, Jack Blott, Frank Cappon and Harry Kipke inspect a pair of Little Brown Jugs prior to the 1932 Minnesota game.

Board finally won its turf war with the Regents by the time Michigan returned to the conference, but the victory came with a price.

Law professor Ralph W. Aigler saved the Board from obscurity, and served as its chairman from 1915 to 1955. With his new authority he also saved Yost's program from being undermined, and spearheaded Michigan's return to the Big Ten. Years later, however, Professor Aigler would use his power to engineer Yost's demise.

Politics behind him, Yost immediately reclaimed Michigan's dominance over the conference in 1918, its first season back. His players zipped through their five-game schedule (shortened by three games due to the national flu epidemic) without a loss.

They gave up only six points all year, and scored satisfying wins over their old rival Chicago and their new rival, Ohio State. By season's end, most sportswriters around the country believed either Michigan or Pop Warner's Pitt team was the nation's best.

Yost's second honeymoon with the Big Ten ended even sooner than his first. In 1919 the Wolverines limped home with a 3-4-1 record, including bitter losses to all four of its biggest foes: Chicago, Ohio State, Illinois and Minnesota, which took home the Brown Jug for the first time. The poor showing stuck them in seventh place. In Yost's 29-year coaching career, this would be his only losing season.

The on-field setback coincided with Yost's off-field misfortunes. His Tennessee business ventures hit their lowest point, while in Ann Arbor Yost was engaged in a political struggle over who would lead the new physical education department. Yost, naturally, wanted to head the new division, but President Burton warned him, "If I gave this work to you the campus would blow up."

In addition to these thorns in Yost's side, he heard predictable grumbling about his competence as coach. At one time the U-M Alumni Club of Grand Rapids sent a formal request for Yost's resignation. The backlash against the club was so great, including hundreds of letters, petitions and denouncements, that Yost cracked, "I ought to erect a monument to those Grand Rapids alumni. If it hadn't been for them, I might never have known how many friends I had and how loyal they are, both to myself and to Michigan."

Yost toyed with the idea of quitting to attend to his flagging business interests, but he chose instead to rededicate himself to Michigan. President Burton, recognizing Yost's popularity, compromised by splitting the physical education position in two and giving Yost half. His title, "Director of Intercollegiate Athletics," is what we now call Athletic Director. The new job increased Yost's salary and, more importantly, it gave him a reason to live in Ann Arbor year-round.

To return Michigan to its former glory, Yost reverted to his old "Hurry Up" self once more. He urged the student newspaper, the fraternities and alumni to get more good athletes out for the team, and received an avalanche of help.

1936
With Columbia's
Lou Little

Recruiting was much simpler back then, with almost all the players coming from Michigan or Ohio. The game wasn't nearly as specialized as it is now, either, so a good athlete could easily be taught the game of football. Players were given scholarships sight-unseen, walk-ons became standouts, and three-sport stars were common. Thus, Yost's plea for help could net quick results.

With a beefed up squad, Michigan went 5-2 in 1920 and 5-1-1 in 1921, then shifted back into overdrive with undefeated seasons in 1922 and 1923. This renaissance might have been Yost's best coaching. Not only did he pick the team up from the middle of the pack, he did so within the new conference rules.

When one of the alums Yost solicited to help rebuild the team was rumored to have gone too far in enticing men to play at Michigan, Yost cut him off, and fast. Yost then addressed the Detroit alumni chapter to underscore his revised opinion that it was better to keep Michigan's name clean and lose than to cut corners and win. Yost had finally transferred his long-standing belief in clean play on the field to disciplined conduct off it.

According to Edwin Pope, "Yost never needed an eligibility committee in his early days. He completely disregarded rules in early talent searches. Later he regretted his carelessness and became an advocate of stringent scholastic standards for athletes. But he never liked to be kidded about these violations."

Ironically, the only whiff of scandal Yost ever suffered occurred after he had made this philosophical shift. The comprehensive Carnegie

Yost at a reunion with his former boss, Charles Baird (left), and former U-M trainer Keene Fitzpatrick.

Report, published in 1929, studied more than a hundred college football programs. In the process they suggested Michigan bent recruiting rules when Yost was head coach. They acknowledged that no Michigan coaches ever initiated contact with a recruit — one of the new NCAA rules at the time — but the report said Michigan's coaches encouraged alumni to tell high school players to write to the coaches, which then allowed them to write back. By modern standards the charge seems absurd, but it was taken seriously by all involved, especially Yost.

In its defense, Michigan received help from a surprising source: Major John L. Griffith, the Big Ten commissioner. He pointed out significant errors in the report, and wondered how Iowa could be given "a clean bill of health" when they had just been suspended from the Big Ten for nine months for serious violations, while Michigan was taken to task in the report for relatively minor infractions. The commissioner wrote:

"I always come away from Michigan with the feeling that you ... have built your own ideals into Michigan's athletics and that everything is on a sane and sound basis. I hardly ever make a talk when I do not mention the things that you are doing. Our colleges and universities may well look to Michigan as an ideal."

Thus, despite Yost's loose interpretation of the off-field rules when he started at Michigan, by the

1920's Michigan's long-standing reputation as a competitive, clean program had begun to take root.

Encore

In 1924, satisfied with his long list of coaching accomplishments and eager to begin building the Michigan athletic empire, Yost stepped down as the football coach. He turned over the duties of head coach to George Little, who had coached successfully at Miami before serving as Yost's assistant football coach and assistant athletic director.

Unfortunately, 1924 started another Michigan tradition: those who follow coaching legends don't fare well. Little performed admirably, going 6-2 overall and 4-2 in the Big Ten. He might have survived the team's fourth-place finish if he hadn't faced Illinois.

1924
During 1-year retirement

The 1924 Illinois team eagerly awaited the Michigan game. The Illini chose to dedicate their new stadium that day, but more importantly, bragging rights were on the line. The previous season the two teams were considered by most experts to be the two best in the nation — but since they didn't play each other, the matter couldn't be decided until 1924.

The Illini settled the matter convincingly. Red Grange and the his teammates steamrolled Michigan, 39-14. No team had scored that many points against the Wolverines in 32 years.

To make matters worse for Little, Yost and his wife traveled to Champaign for that game, and watched Grange bust loose for 409 yards and five touchdowns. More incredibly, Grange covered 262 of those yards in just four runs. Many football historians still consider Grange's effort the greatest single game any football player has ever played.

"Grange scored all those points, but that was not against Fielding Yost," Schembechler exclaims in his office, pointing his finger. While the Yosts watched from the stands, Yost's wife kept nudging him in the ribs, saying, "We can't have this," while gesturing towards the field.

"Yost's up there watching, and Grange runs wild," Schembechler says. "It was just killin' Yost. He called George Little and said, 'I'm coming back!'"

What happened that day is part of college football lore. What happened during the next year's rematch is known by only a few Michigan die-hards.

It's generally assumed Grange's miracle day occurred during his final college season. Not true. Grange was only a junior in 1924, and therefore had to play Michigan again the next season, and again in Champaign. This time, however, he had to face a hungry bunch of Wolverines drilled by Fielding Yost himself.

In 1925, Yost's first year back, Michigan had already beaten Michigan State, Indiana and Wisconsin by a combined score of 123-0 — definitely Yost-style numbers. Yost put Benny Friedman at quarterback and Bennie Oosterbaan everywhere else. With those two all-Americans leading the way, Michigan pulled out a 3-0 victory over the Illini and smothered the "Galloping Ghost." Yost's strategy was simple: make Oosterbaan follow Grange wherever he went, with or without the ball, all day long. Oosterbaan did his job: Grange scrounged only 65 yards on 25 carries — less than 3 per run.

Yost called that 1925 squad his "greatest team ever," which is why the Northwestern game must have been particularly disappointing. The Wolverines entered their sixth game with a 5-0 record and a 180-0 point differential. They would finish at 7-1, outscoring their opponents 227-3. How could they lose? Northwestern scored those three points — on a muddy field at Grant Park that was almost called off due to the horrible weather conditions — which was enough to beat Michigan, 3-2.

Michigan lost just once more in 1926 — to Navy, who would be named national champions at season's end — taking home the Big Ten title two years in a row. Yost ended his coaching career at Michigan the way he started it: with four near-perfect seasons (28-2-1), and four consecutive conference titles.

By the time Yost stepped down as head coach for the second and final time, Big Ten commissioner Griffith was probably right: Michigan actually did represent college football at its best.

The Empire Builder

The minute President Burton named Yost the new athletic director in 1921, he was on a mission to construct the very best athletic complex in the nation, one built to last well into the next millenium. As a coach, Yost's enthusiasm marked his success. As an athletic director, his vision set him apart.

"From 1901 to 1921 Yost did not innovate anywhere but on the field," says Canham. "But for the next 20 years [as athletic director], he was unbelievable."

Yost faced plenty of obstacles, but his three biggest impediments were the administration, funding problems, and his own ego. He managed to overcome the first two, and mitigate the third.

"They didn't want him as athletic director, because he was so much his own man," Canham says. "His ego got in the way. He was very worried about what appeared in the paper about him, in a way Bo and I never were."

If Yost's ambitious proposals were subject to University politics, he wouldn't have won many

battles, and he probably knew it. To insulate him from clashes with the administrators, Yost used the Faculty Board in Control of Athletics as his foil. If he agreed with somone, he'd tell them himself; but if he disagreed, he'd claim the issue was out of his hands because, hey, the Board had jurisdiction over the matter. Yost somehow neglected to mention that he, in turn, effectively ran the Board.

"From Yost to Crisler to me, we had a Faculty Board in Control, and the presidents we served under believed that faculty control was the way to control athletics," Canham says today. "Yost easily controlled the faculty committee. He was the first athletic director who really benefitted from having the faculty in control, and without that, he'd never be able to do what he did. Yost had support from the Board for the same reason I did: he never took stupid things to them (for approval)."

By the time Yost became athletic director in 1921, the Regents had little power over the Board members, but the Board still answered to the president. Fortunately for Yost, during the first 10 years of his term as athletic director he served under four presidents, none of whom were around long enough to resist Yost's massive building campaign.

Only one president, Alexander Ruthven, served longer than five years "under Yost." But Ruthven's term ran from 1929 to 1951, starting a year after Yost had completed most of his buildings and ending 10 years after Yost's retirement. Further, since Ruthven knew almost nothing about sports, he wasn't about to challenge the highly popular, knowledgable Yost. If Yost served under a hardnosed, involved president like James B. Angell, Michigan's athletic campus might look very different today.

"Yost was lucky, very lucky, that he had Alexander Ruthven for a president," Canham says. "Ruthven was a great delegator."

The university presidents stayed out of Yost's way, and the Board rubber stamped Yost's grand plans, but it was the athletic department's financial autonomy that fueled his unprecedented building program.

"He fought to keep the money made in the athletic department in the athletic department, so he had the money to get it done," Kip Taylor says. "*That's how he did it.* Otherwise, if the administration had a choice between spending money on a nurse's dorm on the Hill or a stadium, where do you think it's going?"

The First Bricks

Securing the money for the athletic complex took cunning, but building a sporting nirvana took vision. Within months of taking office Yost started work on his first project, which would be called Yost Field House. Yost's first task was convincing people they needed such a thing.

In 1921, the Michigan athletic complex could hardly be called a complex: it was merely a loose collection of open-aired, temporary structures. Michigan had 42,000-seat Ferry Field, but no golf course, hockey rink or basketball arena. They had a rickety baseball park, no facility to practice any varsity sport indoors, and only one place for students to exercise, tiny Waterman Gym, but that was overcrowded with P.E. classes, students and faculty. Michigan people didn't have much, but they didn't know they needed more until Yost came along.

"Yost said, 'We're going to build this huge building to practice in. Yeah, we can make the roof big enough to punt in,' " Kip Taylor recalls. "And people figured, he's off his rocker. 'All it is is a field with a house over it — so let's call it a field house. Let's make that Yost Field House.' Yeah, the guy's definitely off his rocker, they said. But everyone in the country has a Yost Field House now."

Most pioneers have either great vision or a great

1910
Game program

eye for detail. Yost had an overabundance of both. After imagining what the nation's most advanced athletic facility would look like, he dove into the practical matters with his characteristic obsessiveness. His close work with the engineers, financiers and builders impressed them all. Yost even toured the Ohio company that made the bricks to make certain they would be good enough for Yost Field House.

"Details, details, details," Canham says. "Yost watched everything."

The name of the building didn't escape Yost's attention, either. He coined the term "field house," and naturally wanted it named after himself. Problem was, the university had a policy against naming buildings after living people, so Yost did what he always did when he faced resistance: he rounded up the students (4,000 of whom signed a petition to name the building after Yost), the alumni, Board members and sympathetic reporters to make his case for him. As usual, the administration buckled. Since then, the university has broken the "no living legacies" rule for Crisler Arena, Canham Natatorium and Schembechler Hall.

When they finished Yost Field House it was by far the biggest building on campus, dwarfing everything near it in early photographs. The raves poured in. A notice in the Detroit Athletic Club News called the new field house "the finest plant of its kind in the world. ... The building will be a monument to (Yost's) belief in the university, and his business sagacity."

Yost made just one mistake. In 1921, the builders estimated the field house would cost $225,000, but when they finished in 1923 the price had more than doubled to $563,000. Instead of calling it a failure, Yost used the deficit to spring-board his next project. He figured the best way to pay off the debt would be to increase football receipts — and the only way to do that was to increase Michigan's seating capacity.

The Big House

When Yost arrived in Ann Arbor the Wolverines played their games where Schembechler Hall is located now, at the 15,500-seat Regents Field. A few years later alumnus Dexter Ferry donated the rest of the huge plot of land that's bordered by State, Stadium, Hoover and the railroad tracks. The university renamed the whole area Ferry Field, and in 1906 moved the football stadium where the outdoor track is now. They built 21,000 seats around the field, then doubled the capacity in 1922.

Nonetheless, it bothered Yost's political instincts that Michigan still couldn't provide enough tickets for state legislators and other power-brokers for the big games. It bothered Yost's pride that other, "lesser" universities like Illinois and Ohio State already had gleaming new super stadiums that could hold more than 70,000. Yost was obsessed with stadiums. The first 11 photos in his 1905 book are not of plays or players but of the nation's best stadiums.

By the mid-1920's Yost had grown sure of two things: he needed to sell more than 40,000 tickets to fund his building program, and there was plenty of demand to sell more. There just weren't enough seats.

Yost had enough sense to know he couldn't pitch the idea of a new stadium to the university as a money-maker. That became clear when an administrative higher-up told Yost the Regents would object to his stadium plans, because they felt that

1926
Game program

"amateur college contests should not be transformed into public spectacles" — a laughable notion today.

Instead of mounting a frontal attack, Yost couched the stadium proposal in a long list of improvements to benefit "Athletics-for-All," a hot movement in the 1920's. On his list of "immediate and pressing needs" to meet this new demand, Yost buried "Increased seating capacity for football stands" midway down his 10-point list, though it was surely the item he cared about most.

Yost bolstered the "Athletics-for-All" angle by writing alumni to promote the idea of entertainment for the masses, not just the students. "Does the university owe any obligation or duty to the alumni and citizens and taxpayers of the state who own and maintain the university?" Yost asked rhetorically. "Should these people who might want to attend the games be taken into consideration in making plans for a stadium?"

Predictably, Yost got backing from students and alumni. He also dropped the names of his many friends in the state legislature when it helped his cause, pointing out that the politicians who decided how much to give the university were often upset that they couldn't get tickets for the games at Ferry Field, and wasn't that a shame?

Once Yost got his way, he shifted his talents from politics to financing. To cover the gap left by the university and state legislature, Yost sold bonds to boosters with his typical flair for promotion. Through his connections with the I.R.S., he managed to get them declared tax-deductible. (A few dozen of these bonds can still be found in some Ann Arbor attics, but the owners don't dare cash them in for the $500.)

Regent's Field, Michigan's first stadium, was the home of the Wolverines from 1893 to 1905.

Yost actually wanted to build a 140,000-seat stadium, but settled for a capacity of 70,000 with 15,000 temporary bleachers and room to expand. They installed 22 miles of California redwood for the seats, and planted a single four-leaf clover for good luck.

Though almost all fields ran east-west at the time, Yost designed Michigan Stadium to run north-south. This kept the sun out of the players' eyes and the fall winds to a minimum, which run east-west. Today, all football fields do it Yost's way. He also had the foresight to install footings for a second deck (which could still be built today), and, incredibly, to make eight large conduits in the cement to handle the wiring necessary for electronic media.

"Yost knew there was something electronic coming," says Howard King, the stadium public address announcer. Today ABC-TV and ESPN use the conduits — still sufficient, even now — that Fielding Yost planned in 1925.

Those conduits weren't the only reason many people thought Yost's new stadium was crazy. "It was the biggest damn hole in the ground I ever saw," says Kip Taylor, who scored the first touchdown in the Big House. "People said, 'Oh, man, Yost is off his rocker.' "

As the workers dug down they ran into countless springs. The workers were frantic. They pleaded with Yost, "We can't control it!" But Yost

Above, Michigan defeated Chicago, 22-0, in 1904 to win their fourth straight national championship.

calmly responded, "Don't let that bother you — we can use that water." The workers asked him where they could possibly use all that water, to which Yost said: "For our golf course right across the street." The workers looked at each other and shook their heads — there was no golf course across the street — so Yost built that golf course, which still depends on the stadium springs for much of its water supply to this day.

With Yost taking the lead, everyone involved in the project worked furiously. They broke ground on Sept. 15, 1926, and hosted the inaugural game just over a year later, on Oct. 1, 1927. Hurry up, indeed.

Michigan Stadium today is the largest college-owned stadium in the country. With a capacity of 102,501, the building could play host to the entire population of Ann Arbor until just a few years ago. It's attracted more than 100,000 fans for every game since Nov. 8, 1975. With those kind of numbers no one questions why Michigan has such an incredible facility, even though it only makes money six days a year. But why did the university build such a monstrosity way back in 1927, when the population of the students and city combined barely topped 35,000? Such extravagance would be equivalent to building a stadium today to seat 325,000 people. The two-word answer: Fielding Yost.

When Michigan sold all 85,000 seats at five bucks a head for the 1927 dedication game against

Ferry Field, completed in 1906, originally seated 18,000 but grew to a capacity of 40,000 in the early 1920's.

Ohio State, Yost was vindicated.

Yost could have quieted the critics who thought U-M sports were getting too big by asking for less. Instead, Yost somehow managed to quiet them down by asking for more.

To offset the largess of Yost Field House and Michigan Stadium, Yost proposed doing more for the forgotten small-sport athletes. In addition to converting a roller-skating facility into an ice rink (still called the Coliseum), Yost built a modern women's gym — well ahead of its time — a new baseball park, dozens of tennis courts and a state-of-the-art golf course designed by Alistair MacKenzie, the same architect who created Augusta National and Pebble Beach.

Yost also built the nation's biggest intramural building, a gorgeous, neo-classical structure that housed 24 racquetball courts (some have since been converted for weight training), four basketball courts and a pool. "It's still a very sound building," says Robert Fox, current director of the Intramural (I.M.) Building. "It has everything in it a modern building has — except maybe a juice bar."

Canham calls the I.M. Building "one of Yost's greatest contributions. Look at all the I.M. buildings across the country — that's because of Yost."

By 1929, Big Ten commissioner Major John L. Griffith was moved to write Yost, "You have built the finest athletic plant in the world."

Few would argue with that statement then. Or now.

Coaching Rivals, Inside and Out

Just because Yost had quit coaching the Wolverines didn't mean he quit watching them. And he didn't always like what he saw.

Tad Wieman played for Yost in the late 1910's. In 1927 Wieman became the second man to try to

1922 team. Against Ohio State that year he ran for one 26-yard touchdown, intercepted a pass for a 38-yard touchdown and kicked a 37-yard field goal. To cap off his remarkably versatile performance, Kipke averaged 47 yards on 11 punts, nine of which he planted inside the Buckeyes' 8-yard line.

Kipke kept up his winning ways when he took over the Michigan coaching duties. After posting a 5-3-1 record in 1929, his rookie season, the highly regarded Kipke captured four consecutive Big Ten titles and two national crowns.

The honeymoon ended in 1934, when the team scored only 21 points the entire year. Their 1-7 record, and last place in the Big Ten, gave the alumni quarterbacks fodder for complaint. The following three seasons, Kipke could only manage nine wins against 15 losses, which did him in.

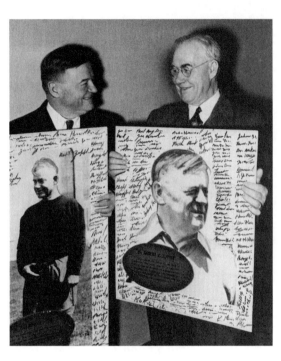

**1942
With Illinois coach
Bob Zuppke**

When the Board released Kipke, the press exhumed their old suspicion that Yost meddled in the coach's efforts, but Kipke flatly refuted the speculation publicly. President Ford himself asserts that, finally, Yost was innocent of that charge.

Ford played for three years under Kipke, two of them for national championship teams, the third for for Kipke's seventh-place 1934 squad. "Yost was athletic director then, but he used to be around the practice field every day," Ford recalls. "He had that cigar flipping around in his mouth, and he had that crazy hat on all the time. But he never interjected himself. He always used good judgment in letting Coach Kipke run practice."

Yost remedied his former tendency to look over his coach's shoulder, which helped Kipke, but he also became more dogged about rule compliance, which hurt Kipke. Yost learned of possible rules violations regarding Kipke's spring practice, some "no-work" summer jobs and alumni funds used to attract recruits — minor stuff in Yost's early coaching days, but intolerable in the 1930's. Those infractions accelerated Kipke's departure.

Yost overcame his rivalry with his own coaches — by the time Crisler took over for Kipke in 1938, Yost was completely hands-off — but his relations with Stagg and Knute Rockne, Notre Dame's legendary coach, never improved much.

Yost bought Stagg's book, *Treatise on Football*, when it came out in 1893 and read it copiously. Yost clearly respected Stagg and what he'd accomplished — which is exactly why he wanted to beat him. Yost, being Yost, didn't set out to do it quietly, either. During his Point-a-Minute years, Yost beat Stagg in their first four showdowns by the combined score of 93-12, including three shutouts. Adding insult to injury, Yost's 1905 book on football was clearly modeled on Stagg's — and got a lot more attention. Yost sent free copies to newspapers, in return for reviews like this one from The New York Evening Mail: "Coach Yost is recognized as the greatest coach in the West and some even give him the palm for all-America." Such reports must have burned the prideful Stagg.

"These two were never on the best of terms," wrote Will Perry, the long-time Michigan sports

Yost's Michigan Stadium opened in 1927 seating 84,000-plus. It was later expanded to seat 102,501.

replace Yost since the ill-fated George Little left town after the Red Grange debacle. Unfortunately for Wieman, his efforts seemed sabotaged from the start.

He learned just two weeks before the first game of 1927 that he would be the head coach, but he started out very strong, shutting out his first four opponents. After losses to Illinois and Minnesota, however, Wieman finished with a 6-2 record and third place in the Big Ten. It was not the stuff legends are made of, but it seemed good enough to keep the faithful from rioting.

Nonetheless, before the 1928 season the papers reported rumors that Yost would be head coach that season. Although Wieman ultimately performed all the duties of head coach that year, in the papers Yost coyly played both sides of the issue, which kept the controversy alive.

The team lost its first four games and finished

seventh in the Big Ten.

After the season Wieman wrote Yost a number of very respectful letters, merely asking for clarification of the coaching situation. Yost responded by firing him.

After one year away from the game, Wieman resurfaced as line coach for the Minnesota Gophers, who happened to be coached by Mr. Fritz Crisler. It doesn't take a genius to imagine Wieman and Crisler talking about Mr. Wieman's former employer, which no doubt affected the future relationship between Crisler and Yost.

As inexcusable as his treatment of Wieman was, Yost's most surprising quality was his ability to correct past faults. In 1929 Yost named Harry Kipke the next Michigan coach. Yost and the players had ample reason to respect the new coach. Kipke earned nine letters in football, basketball and baseball, and all-American status on Yost's undefeated

Yost competes in a curling tournament at the Detroit Athletic Club in 1940.

Yost greets Amos Alonzo Stagg with a gift of an Indian headress at a U-M halftime ceremony.

information director. Stagg got the last laugh, when he fashioned the Big Ten rules that kept Michigan out of the conference for 10 years.

Kip Taylor maintains, however, that the two coaches respected each other, they just couldn't show it. He might be right. Yost saved a 1922 clipping from a Detroit paper, in which the 61-year-old Stagg told his critics who were asking him to resign, "You can tell those fellows to come out here 10 years from now if they're still alive, and they'll find me on the job." Clearly, the clip must have meant something to Yost for him to save it to his death.

Yost's relations with Chicago could be considered downright chummy compared to his relations with Notre Dame. Yost's teams played Notre Dame three times early in his career (winning two and losing one), but they soon cut short the series, despite their obvious similarities.

Yost probably didn't like all the attention Notre Dame received, especially for things Yost properly deserved the credit for, like popularizing the forward pass. Notre Dame and Michigan also argued over whether Notre Dame should have had to comply with Big Ten off-field rules to play those teams. According to John Kryk's *Natural Enemies*, at one point Notre Dame was so upset about being ostracized by Big Ten schools that it applied for admission, and was rejected. Finally, in 1912, Notre Dame made what Kryk calls "the most crucial decision in the history of Notre Dame athletics" – It would abide by the highest standards, including the Big Ten's eligibility rules.

Right when things were getting better, Yost made them worse. During these years Yost picked a respected all-American team; in 1913, he named three of his players to the squad, and not one player

Yost visits with his former star players, Germany Schulz (middle) and Willie Heston (right), in 1939.

from Notre Dame. One of those snubbed players never forgot it: Knute Rockne.

With this backdrop, Yost-Rockne relations seemed doomed from the start. Yet with a concerted effort at diplomacy from both sides, the two famous coaches were amicable during the first few years of Rockne's career as coach of the Irish in the early 1920's. At one coaches' conference the two legends swapped stories long after the others had gone home.

All that changed during a 1923 track meet in Ann Arbor. Though it was officially a Big Ten meet, the informality of the times allowed Michigan to invite a few non-conference schools like Notre Dame. Michigan battled closely with Illinois for the championship when an Illini runner seemed to clinch the title for his school by winning the 120-yard high hurdles.

However, seconds after the race someone pointed out that the third hurdle in each lane was off by several feet, disturbing the runners' strides. Estimates of the gap ranged from five feet to eight inches, depending on who was doing the measuring. The meet referee ordered the race run again, which the Illini refused. Obviously, this would have had no effect on Michigan-Notre Dame relations, until several schools withdrew in support of Illinois — led by Notre Dame track coach Knute Rockne.

The hurdle results were eventually thrown out altogether, which gave Michigan the title by a narrow margin. The track dispute itself died down, but not before ripping apart the delicate bond between Rockne and Yost. The Michigan coach used the event as an opportunity to deride the Fighting Irish as traitors, rule-breakers and worse. Rockne was stunned, and returned a few jabs of his own.

Yost and his wife, Eunice, at their Ann Arbor home in 1944.

The personal animosity between the two titans remained at a fever pitch for years. When a Spalding salesman once tried to get Rockne to place an order for new equipment, Rockne kept repeating that he was overstocked with everything he needed. Finally, the clever salesman said, just before turning to go, that it was a shame because Yost liked Spalding's new footballs so much he'd ordered three dozen.

"He did?" Rockne snapped. "Then I'll take three

dozen and a half."

It took years for the reputation of Notre Dame to recover from Yost's charges. The truth is, Rockne's young program probably was more lax initially than others in the 1920's, especially in terms of recruiting and eligibility. In the 1970's Notre Dame legend Frank Leahy said, "Rockne did things recruiting that would appall a modern coach," though the exact same thing could be said of Yost's early practices. The Rockne-Yost rift continued right up to Rockne's death in an airplane crash on March 31, 1931.

Afterwards, Yost gushed in the papers that Rockne-coached teams "played clean, hard, fast, versatile football and were never beaten until the last whistle. ... Rockne has done more than any other single man to attract general interest to the game." Yost's keen sense for public relations probably compelled the comments — or perhaps it was his guilt over starting and maintaining the battle with Rockne — but it's also true that Yost's compliments were accurate.

In typical Yost fashion, he overcome his old prejudice and accepted Notre Dame's peace offering in the late 1930's. By 1939 Notre Dame's No. 1 enemy had committed his school to play the Irish in 1942 and 1943.

Yost surprised them all again.

A Peculiar Institution

It could be argued that most of Yost's faults were benign flaws, maybe even necessary evils. But one of Yost's blind-spots had no redeeming qualities: he was a racist.

When Ann Arbor High's own George Jewett earned his third varsity letter on the Michigan football team in 1892, he could not have known it would take 40 years for another black player to earn the next one. (In fairness, it should be noted that the university enrolled very few blacks in those days. As late as 1938, of the 1,310 senior photographs in the school yearbook, only three students are black. Nonetheless, there is no question the complete absence of blacks on Yost's teams was intentional.)

The man who finally repeated Jewett's accomplishment was an exemplary man in many ways. Willis Ward graduated near the top of his Detroit Northwestern class, performed at a world-class level in sports, and enjoyed the respect of those who knew him. Still, to get him on the Michigan team Kipke reportedly came close to a fist-fight

with Yost in his office. With the considerable support of Kipke and others, Ward made the team in 1932 and even earned honorable mention on the all-America team the next year.

The 1934 season halted Ward's progress. Michigan scheduled Georgia Tech at home for the third game of the season. At that time no Southern schools allowed blacks on their teams, nor played teams which did. So, when a Northern team played a Southern team, it was customary for the Northern team to bench its black players. The Southern team, in turn, would bench players of comparable skill to compensate.

Complicating matters, the Georgia Tech coach, Bill Alexander, was a good friend of Dan McGugin, who was Yost's brother-in-law and closest friend. McGugin played for Yost's first teams in Ann Arbor, he married Yost's sister-in-law, he entered into many business ventures with his former coach and lived in the same town — Nashville — as Yost for nine months a year until Yost become athletic director. In the meantime, with Yost's help, McGugin became Vanderbilt's head coach, where he compiled a Yost-like record of 197-55-19. (McGugin's mark still dwarfs that of the second-best coach in Vanderbilt's history, who won 39 games while losing 54.) Since Yost and the Georgia Tech coach shared such a close mutual friend, Yost felt further compelled to bench Ward for the game.

The attention Yost's decision received surprised and embarrassed him. In his limited view of the situation, Yost thought he was simply providing a courtesy for a friend, not making a racial stand. National newspapers, radio programs and even *Time* magazine featured the controversy prominently. It also sparked bitter debate among students, and created a morale problem on the team. By all accounts the players felt Ward was intelligent, hard-working and well-liked.

One of those players was Jerry Ford, who roomed with Ward on the road. "Willis was probably my

What if Yost were around today? "He'd probably take credit for everything," says former U-M athletic director Don Canham, "and he'd probably be right. He's like the guy who invented the automobile: there have been a lot of cars built since, but only one guy who did it first. Yost was an absolute genius in the field he chose to work in. He made the foundation here, and as a result, the foundation of athletics across the country."

closest friend on the football team," Ford says today. "Willis and I were the leaders of the team."

According to a story that was scheduled to appear in *The Ann Arbor Observer* in the fall of 1996, "Ford agonized over whether he should play, quit the team or just what he should do." Ford recalled that Ward "urged me to play for the benefit of the team, so I did."

The team notched its only victory of the season against Georgia Tech, 9-2, but they were never the same after that. "The team was hurt," Ward said in 1983. "It was a horrible thing."

"Our morale certainly wasn't made any better," Ford says. "We had a terrible time."

Though Canham feels its generally unfair to judge his predecessors without considering the times they lived in, he is convinced that "Pulling Willis Ward out of the (Georgia Tech) game was bad. (Yost) should have known better by then. I think Yost got caught up with his friends in the South. But the negative PR from that incident opened up opportunities for blacks in the future."

Despite Yost's error in judgment, Ward believed Yost had successfully "flip-flopped from being a segregationist" two years earlier when Ward made the team.

Ward recalled his first trip to Chicago with the team in 1932. At the time, black players usually stayed with local families because the pricier hotels still did not accept black guests. Sure enough, when the team tried to check in, the hotel manager told Yost they did not admit blacks, and they weren't about to start now. According to Ward, Yost became outraged.

" 'We've been staying at this hotel since 1900,' " Ward recalled Yost saying, " 'and we'll pull every

(Michigan) team and I'll get other Big Ten teams to not stay here!' "

The angry appeal to their financial interest was enough to desegregate the hotel for one night. Ward became only the second African-American to stay in the hotel, the first being Marian Anderson.

There are other examples of Yost's surprising change of heart from his racist past. He successfully lobbied to get black track star DeHart Hubbard into the university; he volunteered his influence and Field House to support an athletic exhibition to raise funds for the Dunbar Center, a local organization that promoted social betterment for African-Americans; and he started Benny Friedman, a practicing Jew, at quarterback in the mid-1920's, then helped him become athletic director at Brandeis University. This is not to suggest Yost became a pillar of social justice. But, for the son of a Confederate soldier born six years after the Civil War, the examples above do indicate Yost at least recognized the changing times, and had begun to change with them.

Incidentally, Ward and Ford remained close friends until Ward's death in 1983. When Ward once ran for Congress, Ford left his own campaign in Grand Rapids to stump for Ward, and later endorsed his nomination for a position on the bench. According to Ford, "Willis turned out to be an excellent state judge."

When Yost retired in 1941, he had not only established an examplary record as an athletic coach and empire builder, he had become serious about following off-field rules, leaving his coaches alone, and sloughing his discriminatory practices.

Nonetheless, Ralph Aigler, the same law professor who restored the authority of the Board and

1941
at retirement

lead the effort to return to the Big Ten, painfully undermined Yost in his last years. Although Yost actively courted Navy coach Tom Hamilton to replace Kipke for the 1938 season, Aigler secretly offered the job to a reluctant Fritz Crisler, then coaxed him to accept it. Crisler proved a savvy choice, but the process emasculated Yost.

Yost's final years were sad ones.

No Place to Hurry To

In 1942, a young Wolverine high-jumper named Don Canham and his teammates traveled to the University of Illinois campus for the Big Ten track meet. On the train coming back from Champaign, Canham sat up all night talking with Fielding Yost himself.

"He was very egotistical, always talking about what he'd done," Canham says. "He was a bull in a china shop. Listening to him that night, you could see he couldn't imagine he wouldn't get his own way on everything. He just felt he owned it. I can't remember much of what we talked about, but I recall he talked about Michigan until it was coming out your ears."

Such nights were, sadly, the highlights of Yost's final years. When Aigler offered Crisler the coaching job without Yost's knowledge, it was clear Yost no longer ran the athletic department. But, uncharacteristically, Yost did not raise a ruckus, and stepped aside graciously.

As he approached retirement, his admirers helped rekindle old memories by hosting a few banquets for him. One of the more spectacular tributes was titled "A Toast to Yost from Coast to Coast," the same title of a popular song. NBC radio broadcast 30 minutes of Yost's boosters paying homage to the legend, including Senator Arthur Vandenberg, the Big Ten commissioner, university presidents, famous poets and celebrities like Branch Rickey and Illinois coach Bob Zuppke, right alongside hundreds of Yost's former players like Willie Heston, Germany Schulz and the "two

Bennies," Friedman and Oosterbaan. Heston was moved to say, "He was like a father to me." In their statements and letters, it's clear Yost's players remained loyal to the end.

When Yost retired in 1941, the university gave him the title of Professor Emeritus and a room in Yost Field House. His office was neat and tidy, but filled with team photos on the wall, trophies on the tables and a replica of the Little Brown Jug on his desk. Yost still wore a suit and tie every day, with his straight white hair swept across his forehead. Yost also sported wire-rimmed glasses and a humble expression — something you never see in earlier photos — which gave him the dapper, friendly aura of Mr. Chips.

Don Lund played on the football and baseball teams then, which frequently took him past Yost on his way to indoor practices. "I'd go by and see him in his office at the Field House," Lund recalls, "I saw an older man, just sort of fiddling around with papers on his desk."

Yost didn't have much to do except answer his correspondence. He continued to receive stacks of mail until his death, and answered all letters with remarkable promptness and good cheer. He even took his correspondence with him when he traveled just to keep up.

Yost tried to keep busy at home, too. "The doctors told Yost not to shovel his driveway, so he hired us to do it," remembers Al Gallup, whose best childhood friend lived next door to Yost. "But he was so particular, or restless, that in the process of showing us exactly how he wanted it done he pretty much shoveled the whole thing off himself."

Another time Gallup and his friend were flying a kite in front of Yost's house. He came outside to show them how to really do it, but the second he grabbed the string it went crashing behind his house. He was nice enough to buy them a new one.

Crisler respected Yost and his accomplishments but kept him at a distance — perhaps wisely. As a result, Yost had little to do. When Schembechler hears these stories of his predecessor, he shudders a bit. "I hope I don't end up like that," he says quietly, thinking out loud. "Nowadays there's this glorification of coaches and they have extreme popularity that we probably don't deserve. But back then, they didn't make as big a fuss."

There were no book signings for old coaches in the 1940's, no speaking tours or endorsement deals. Just memories.

"When the old man retired, I used to feel extremely sorry for him," Kip Taylor says. "He built the whole thing, and now he had nothing to say about it, nothing to do with it. I felt so sad for him. He just wanted someone to talk to, but they put him on a shelf, no one wanted to talk to him. Whenever someone stopped by to talk football, he perked up. He'd always been the front man, but now he felt left out. He was a lost soul. That was his life, you see.

"I felt so sad for him," Taylor says again, voice drifting off.

Yost was 70 years old when he retired and was still eager to Hurry Up, but he had no place to hurry to. The idleness, the lack of purpose, eroded him.

With little to do, and no one to talk to, Yost would leave his office in the afternoon to go for walks in the streets of the university campus — the way he used to when he coached the Point-a-Minute teams. He'd often seek out the Sigma Chi fraternity to talk with the boys about Meeshegan football. Sometimes he became lost, disoriented, and kept wandering about until someone back at the office asked, "Where's Fielding?" and started looking for him. The Ann Arbor police often found him; they'd pick him up, coax him into their car, and return him to his home tucked back in the woods by the river.

What he longed for, more than anything, was to be "Fielding Yost" again, to be able walk into a local shop, discuss last weekend's game, and have everyone listen. But those days were over.

"If the old man were to walk in here right now," Kip Taylor speculated, sitting in an Ann Arbor restaurant, "he'd light up, seeing a few Michigan men talking about Michigan football, and sit down and join us."

"Fielding Yost Hung His Hat Here"

Yost was born six years after the Civil War and died one year after World War II, on Oct. 20, 1946. A year later, Fritz Crisler's national championship team helped make the final payments on the "House that Yost Built" – Michigan Stadium.

Yost's son, Buck, outlived his father but not his mother. When Mrs. Yost died in the early 1970's, no other family members remained. Millie Schembechler, the new First Lady of Michigan Football, handled her funeral arrangements.

In addition to his small family, Yost left behind the greatest legacy in college football. The records of his Point-a-Minute teams remain the greatest of this century. His all-time winning percentage is still the highest of any coach with at least 25 years experience. Yost's innovations, including pre-season conditioning, the spiral, the linebacker and the fake kick — are still at the center of football today.

Notre Dame coach Lou Holtz is respected as a genuine student of college football. Though clearly partial to Knute Rockne, he recognizes Yost's high station in the game's history. "Yost would win today," Holtz says, "because he could communicate with people, he was innovative, and competitive."

Yost's building program remains unequaled, anywhere. The Michigan teams for football, golf and baseball still play on the fields that Yost built. "He dreamt of the greatness that could be Michigan," Taylor says. "He didn't make temporary buildings. Those were built to last."

The Field House named after him is now home to the Michigan hockey team — an adaptation that probably would have thrilled Yost. He'd be even more excited to hear the Michigan hockey players won the NCAA championship, and that Brendan Morrison, the team's star from Western Canada, said, "I think Yost is the best rink in college hockey."

Yost enjoys a spirited track meet at Ferry Field in 1941, his final year as U-M's athletic director.

For all its modern amenities, Crisler Arena doesn't have half the soul of Yost's buildings.

More than his plays, more than his buildings, Yost gave college football a measure of respectability it never had before. When Yost successfully argued sports can instill vital qualities in students that the classroom cannot, he helped usher athletics into the mainstream of respectable society. When Yost began coaching in 1897, many considered football a game of hooligans; when he retired from sports in 1941, far more considered football the pinnacle of Americans at their best.

Famous sportswriter Grantland Rice once said of Yost: "No other man has ever given as much heart, soul, brains and tongue to the game he loved — football."

And if he were around today? "He'd probably take credit for everything," Canham chuckles, "and he'd probably be right. He's like the guy who invented the automobile: there have been a lot of cars built since, but only one guy who did it first. Yost was an absolute genius in the field he chose to work in. He made the foundation here, and as a result, the foundation of athletics across the country."

After being prompted, Canham speculates: "He'd probably approve of most of what I did, because he was a gambler. I think we'd probably get along pretty well — and I'd remind him of our train trip."

Yost is remembered first and foremost as a Michigan man.

At one of the various banquets for him near the end of his life, Yost said, "My heart is so full at this moment and I am so overcome by the rush of memories that I fear I could say little more. But do let me reiterate ... the Spirit of Michigan. It is based upon a deathless loyalty to Michigan and all her ways; an enthusiasm that makes it second nature for Michigan men to spread the gospel of their university to the world's distant outposts; a conviction that nowhere is there a better university, in any way, that this Michigan of ours."

Yost's greatest legacy might be the people who are still attracted to his vision of Michigan, people who keep coming here to be a part of it years after his death.

When Don Canham became athletic director in 1968, one of his first tasks was to find a new football coach. He called Bo Schembechler, who was making $20,000 a year at Miami. Canham offered $21,000, and Schembechler took it happily. Canham realized Miami could have thrown more money at Schembechler, "but they couldn't compete with Yost's hole in the ground, or with the prestige of Michigan."

Canham knew he was offering something special, and so did Schembechler.

When Schembechler and his staff first arrived in Ann Arbor, they dressed in the second-floor locker room of Yost Field House. They had to sit in rusty, folding chairs and hang their clothes on bolts in the wall.

"My coaches were complaining, 'We had better stuff at Miami,' " Schembechler recalls. "I said, 'No, we didn't. See this chair? Fielding Yost sat in this chair. See this nail on the wall? Fielding Yost hung his hat on this nail. And you're telling me we had better stuff at Miami? No, men, we didn't. We have *tradition* here, Michigan tradition, and that's something no one else has."

Michigan's football tradition: It all started with Yost.

1927
Bronze bust of Yost

Yost's coaching record

Year	Team	W	L	T
1897	Ohio Wesleyan	7	1	1
1898	Nebraska	7	4	0
1899	Kansas	10	0	0
1900	Stanford	7	2	1
1901	Michigan	11	0	0
1902	Michigan	11	0	0
1903	Michigan	11	0	1
1904	Michigan	10	0	0
1905	Michigan	12	1	0
1906	Michigan	4	1	0
1907	Michigan	5	1	0
1908	Michigan	5	2	1
1909	Michigan	6	1	0
1910	Michigan	3	0	3
1911	Michigan	5	1	2
1912	Michigan	5	2	0
1913	Michigan	6	1	0
1914	Michigan	6	3	0
1915	Michigan	4	3	1
1916	Michigan	7	2	0
1917	Michigan	8	2	0
1918	Michigan	5	0	0
1919	Michigan	3	4	0
1920	Michigan	5	2	0
1921	Michigan	5	1	1
1922	Michigan	6	0	1
1923	Michigan	8	0	0
1925	Michigan	7	1	0
1926	Michigan	7	1	0
Total		**196**	**36**	**12**

Fielding Yost's teams won 5 national championships and 14 conference titles (of a possible 19) in 29 seasons.

FRITZ CRISLER

By Angelique S. Chengelis

Genius on the Gridiron

He was an innovator who changed the game in many ways,
but perhaps his most inspired creation was two-platoon football,
which helped define the college and pro game as we now know it.
Of course, fans probably believe Crisler's most indelible mark
was the now-famous maize-and-blue winged helmet.

His players jokingly referred to him as "The Lord", and it is true, Herbert Orin (Fritz) Crisler commanded that kind of respect from colleagues, players and observers of the college game.

Even now, nearly 50 years since he coached his last Michigan team, Fritz Crisler is remembered by his players as one of the greatest influences on their lives. Fans of college football today might not know of Crisler, but certainly, college football is forever indebted to his creative mind.

Most definitely, Crisler, whose glory years in coaching occurred at Michigan from 1938-47, culminating with a national championship, was ahead of his time. He was an innovator who changed the game in so many ways, but perhaps his most inspired creation was two-platoon football, which helped define the college and pro game as we now know it. Of course, Michigan fans probably believe

Crisler's most indelible mark was the now-famous maize-and-blue winged helmet.

Crisler said years after he had completed his service at U-M as football coach, and then as athletic director, that taking the position at Michigan was the best thing that happened to him. It can be argued Crisler was the best thing that happened to Michigan.

In 10 seasons, his Michigan teams went 71-16-3 (.806), including the perfect season and national title in 1947. Of those who coached at Michigan for 10 or more years, Crisler's winning percentage is second to Fielding Yost.

That is a remarkable percentage considering Michigan annually played one of the toughest schedules in the nation. Crisler-coached Michigan teams never dropped out of the Top 20 rankings, and in eight of his 10 seasons, the Wolverines were ranked ninth or better.

Crisler made his mark as an administrator, as well. He became athletic director in 1941, and dur-

Fritz Crisler, seated on second row, far right, played end on the Medotta High School football team.

ing his tenure that lasted 27 years, Michigan teams won 20 all-sports championships in the Big Ten, including nine straight (1942-50).

His reputation led him to the NCAA rules committee, of which he twice served as chairman. His life, though, was devoted to Michigan, and while he will always be noted for his innovations as a football coach, he also was a visionary in terms of campus athletic facilities. Among his biggest improvements were the expansion of Michigan Stadium and construction of the events building that now bears his name, Crisler Arena.

An Unlikely Athlete

That Crisler ever made his way into football is remarkable because he literally stumbled into it.

He was born Herbert Orin to Albert and Catherine, on January 12, 1899. They lived on a farm in Earlville, Ill., a small town of 1,420 located 70 miles west of Chicago. As a youngster he was given the nickname of "Hub."

He was barred from the Earlville High football team in 1913 because he wasn't big enough — he weighed only 92 pounds. There was an old fable that would be told when Crisler's early years were discussed. He was so unathletic and uncoordinated, Crisler and a disabled boy were the only boys in the group of 17 at the school who did not play football. It wasn't until the family moved a year later to the nearby town of Medotta, that

Crisler played end, halfback and quarterback on the University of Chicago varsity football squad.

Crisler was able to distinguish himself athletically. His prowess was on the baseball field, though, not the gridiron.

More importantly, Crisler was a star in the classroom. He knew with the family's limited finances, the only way to further his education was to earn a scholarship. With a high-school average of 94, Crisler made his way to the University of Chicago in 1917, a year that would forever change his life.

When he entered school that fall, Crisler had no intention of getting into athletics. He was going to prepare himself for a career in medicine, following in the footsteps of an uncle who was a physician at Rush Medical Center in Chicago.

Crisler, though, could not resist the temptation of visiting the football team's practice field, and he was impressed as he walked the sideline. There, the legendary Amos Alonzo Stagg, the "Old Man of the Midway" as he was called, was coaching his team.

"I never before had seen the inside of a gymnasium or a college team practice," Crisler recalled in an interview in 1968. "I was just a farm boy looking around. Mr. Stagg, backpedaling away from a play sweeping toward him, bumped into me and we both went down."

The coach and the young student looked at each other.

"Why aren't you out for football?" Stagg said to Crisler.

Crisler earned a total of 9 letters in 3 sports — football, basketball and baseball — while attending Chicago and was offered a pro baseball contract with the Chicago White Sox.

Crisler, here with John Radcliff, played on the 1919-1921 Chicago basketball teams, posting a 54-21 record.

Crisler explained he had never played the game, but Stagg convinced him to attend practice, if only to meet some of his classmates.

He was given a uniform and participated in one practice. It was too much. Without speaking to Stagg, Crisler turned in his uniform and went on his way.

A week later, Stagg was riding his bicycle around campus when he ran into Crisler. He remembered the young man and asked why he had not been back for another practice. Crisler again explained he had little knowledge of football.

"Well, I never thought you'd be a quitter," Stagg said to him.

Stagg's psychological ploy worked, and it was one Crisler often would use later when he coached at Minnesota, Princeton and Michigan.

Stagg was not done with Crisler. During his first scrimmage with the varsity, Crisler bungled the same play three times. Frustrated, Stagg blew his whistle and demanded to know the name of the player who was giving him such a headache. After Crisler gave his name, Stagg asked if he was related to the famous violinist, Fritz Kreisler.

"Kreisler is a gifted, talented artist," Stagg told Crisler. "I'm going to call you Fritz for reasons of contrast, not likeness."

He became Fritz Crisler from that moment on. He also became Stagg's personal favorite, perhaps, in part, for reasons of contrast, not likeness.

After his first season at Chicago, Crisler had to leave college for training in the Infantry Officers' Candidate School at Camp MacArthur in Texas. World War I ended before Crisler could be sent into action, and he was discharged in December 1919, allowing him to return to Chicago, where he would distinguish himself athletically and academically.

Crisler went from having no desire to play any sports in college to playing everything. He won nine letters in three sports — football, basketball and baseball. He attracted attention from major-league scouts for his pitching arm — he was offered a contract with the Chicago White Sox — but football had become Crisler's passion.

He was no longer the tiny kid, undersized and undesirable. Crisler stood 6-foot-2 and was a lean 185 pounds. He was aggressive and smart, and showed off both qualities in a game against Princeton during the 1921 season. It was a performance that would be recognized nationally.

His main position was at end, but Crisler also played at halfback and quarterback, if needed. Princeton boasted a tackle named Stan Keck, who was an enormous 228-pounder with a reputation to match. On the first play, Keck had his way with Crisler, pushing him 5 yards behind the line of scrimmage.

"Milt Romney, our quarterback, picked me up and gave me a look full of reproach," Crisler said in an interview with *The Saturday Evening Post*. "'You're an end,' he told me. 'You're not supposed to be in the backfield. Stay where you belong'"

Crisler responded, and although outsized by about 45 pounds, he literally manhandled Keck. Chicago won the game, 9-0, and Crisler, who later

1928
Assistant at Chicago

called Keck the greatest tackle he had played against, was named by Walter Camp third-team all-American.

In the meantime, Crisler managed to maintain high marks in his academic work, despite playing three sports and working odd jobs. He earned a bachelor's degree in psychology in 1922 and would have received a Phi Beta Kappa key had it not been for a careless freshman. At Chicago, 144 academic points were required for Phi Beta Kappa honors, and Crisler had earned 146, but he was penalized three points for skipping chapel. It was a typical practice of Chicago seniors to coerce a freshman into taking his appointed seat in chapel for roll-call. Crisler's freshman, however, never showed up.

An Assistant to Stagg

Losing out on Phi Beta Kappa honors was the least of Crisler's problems. His cash funds were dwindling, and he decided medical school would have to wait.

Crisler had several options, among them a fellowship in the psychology department at Chicago, but he chose to become Stagg's full-time assistant for football, basketball and baseball. He accepted the position with the understanding he would quit when he had enough money to pursue his medical career. A year later, Crisler was still an assistant to Stagg and, comfortable with his financial security, he married Dorothy Adams on April 12, 1923.

Crisler worked under Stagg for eight years. He watched and listened to the great coach. He took extensive notes and was particularly in tune to how Stagg handled players. There were things about Stagg's coaching style that Crisler did not agree

Crisler assisted Amos Alonzo Stagg at Chicago in football, basketball and track from 1922-1930.

Amos Alonzo Stagg and his top 2 assistants, Fritz Crisler (left) and 'Red' Paine (middle), at a reunion.

with, and he noted in his detailed journals adjustments he would have made. If Crisler had one major complaint with his master, it was the way Stagg ran practices. They often would last five hours and lacked the order and discipline Crisler would later make mandatory when he became a head coach.

It was during these years as understudy that Crisler began developing his own charm and style. One trick he taught himself was that after attending an important business or social function, Crisler would write down all the names of those he met. This way, he would remember them just in case the acquaintance proved useful in the future.

The Offer from Minnesota

In May 1925, after three years as Stagg's assis-

tant, Minnesota athletic director Fred Luehring sent Crisler a Western Union telegram asking him to consider the head-coaching job there. By mid-June, Luehring was ready to hire Crisler, and he was ready to go. Crisler informed Stagg of his desire to take the Minnesota job, but Stagg quickly took the wind out of his sails.

"You're like a bird without feathers or wings," Stagg told him. "You're not ready to fly."

Six days after being offered the Minnesota job, Crisler asked Luehring to withdraw his name.

Crisler stayed with Stagg, knowing the coach would be retiring in 1935 and that he would be the natural successor. But Minnesota came calling again in 1930, and although Crisler immediately thought of turning down the offer, Stagg was the voice of reason this time. Stagg knew backing for athletics at the University of Chicago was dropping off, and he encouraged Crisler to move on.

Stagg was losing his favorite pupil, but as Crisler had learned from his years of training under Stagg, he, too, learned from his student.

"Balance, judgment, dependability and loyalty are his predominant characteristics," Stagg said years later. "In my talks to young people, I have often used him as an illustration of these qualities well-supported by eloquent mental gifts."

Crisler became Minnesota's head coach and athletic director, and he delighted those who had originally hoped for a big-name coach by announcing practices would be open. Crisler also opened his doors for Monday-morning quarterback sessions, allowing fans to voice their suggestions, praise and criticism.

1930
Minnesota coach
————————

It was clear Crisler brought charm and charisma. He bought a new Chevrolet in 1930 — a car he maintained was lucky and kept it for the 18 years he was a college football head coach — and he canvassed the Midwest, preaching the positives of Minnesota football. In his first five months there, he made 103 speeches to Gopher alums, essentially telling them the football program should share equal ground with the school's high academic standards.

The first season was tough, and the Gophers finished 3-4-1, Crisler's only losing season during his lengthy career. Minnesota turned things around in 1931 and went 7-3, including a 6-0 loss at Michigan. Soon after, offers for other head-coaching jobs made their way to Crisler.

The Princeton Challenge

Princeton, like its Ivy League equals, Yale and Harvard, had never hired a non-alumnus to coach football. But Princeton administrators were interested in Crisler and made their bid in 1932. When word leaked of Princeton's interest, the Minnesota students rallied to keep their beloved coach. Crisler kept every letter from every campus group, each having written a petition to keep Crisler. There were petitions signed by the cheerleading squad, the law school council, the dental college, the band and the Minnesota Society of Aeronautic Engineers, to name a few.

Crisler heard the pleas, but Princeton was far too appealing. Here was a chance to prove himself. His task was great, considering the Tigers had won only nine games in the five years before he arrived, but it was exactly the job he sought.

"To be perfectly honest, I fell for the glamour of the Big Three," Crisler had said. "I was flattered as hell that Princeton came after me, a corn-fed yokel, to be its first non-alumnus head coach. What really clinched the decision for me, though, was the obvious fact that all business, publicity and prestige faced east in the early 1930's. Princeton football was in such a mess that it couldn't possibly get worse. It had to improve, and I would get a large share of the credit."

Princeton graduates were not thrilled with the selection of Crisler. But as he had done at Minnesota, Crisler quickly won over his new constituents with his charm. He visited all 85 of the Princeton alumni clubs throughout the nation, and he gave them hope, telling them he would resurrect the program.

Perhaps Crisler's most touchy situation involved the Yale game and what went with it. It was cus-

Walter Hass (left) and Biggie Munn (right) starred for Crisler at Minnesota.

tom that the old Princeton players would return to campus the week of the big game, and they literally, overzealously took over practices. Crisler would have none of that, and he sent the alums into a frenzy when he informed them enough was enough.

Naturally, Crisler had predicted this response, and he had a solution prepared. He gave each of the former players a wallet-sized pass to attend secret practices, with the stipulation they could not divulge the secrets and they must stay on the sidelines. His plan worked, particularly after his team tied Yale, 7-7, in 1932, then defeated the Bulldogs, 27-2, the following year.

Crisler was worked up before his first game against Yale, and every one after that. A frequent caller the night before the game was F. Scott

Fitzgerald, a Princeton graduate, who considered himself a football expert. Fitzgerald occasionally called Crisler at 3 a.m., and he once suggested the key to winning the Yale game would be to capture the team's mascot — the bulldog — which would make the players too distraught to play.

A story written by Fred Russell in *I'll Go Quietly*, a collection of sports stories, not only captured the importance of the Princeton-Yale rivalry, but also the tear-jerking, overly emotional pre-game pep talks for which Crisler was known early in his coaching career.

He had his players seated around him in the locker room, and Crisler spoke solemnly. Players began to sob, and Crisler did likewise. Choking back tears, Russell wrote, Crisler ordered the team to "Go out on that field hallowed by the blood of

Pop Warner (right) and Crisler visit prior to the Minnesota-Stanford game in 1931.

your grandfathers and fight. Tell me as you leave here that you will fight."

Crisler was pleased by the theatrics as his players left the room to take the field. But the second-to-last player walked up to his coach, patted him on the shoulder and said, "Come on, toots, get hold of yourself."

During his first season at Princeton, Crisler would again coach against Michigan. It was the last weekend of October 1932 when the Tigers vis-

ited Ann Arbor, as the Wolverines' Homecoming guest. Harry Kipke was coaching Michigan, which had won five straight. Crisler and his Tigers lost, 14-7, but took solace in the fact the Wolverines eventually went 8-0 and won the national championship.

That was not the only connection with Michigan Crisler would make during his Princeton years. In 1934, he co-authored with former Wolverine player and coach, Tad Wieman, a book called *Prac-*

tical Football. It was the first of two books Crisler would write during his career.

Things improved for Crisler after his first year at Princeton. In six seasons under Crisler, the Tigers were 35-9-5, including unbeaten teams in 1933 and 1935. Both of those teams went 9-0 and were selected as national champions in various polls.

Courted by U-M

By the end of 1937, Crisler's reputation was far-reaching and Michigan came calling.

Dr. Ralph Aigler, dean of Michigan's law school and the university's faculty representative on the Western Conference (Big Ten) committee, sent the first telegram on Dec. 9, 1937, requesting a meeting with Crisler at The Astor Hotel in New York.

They met, and less than a week later, Aigler sent him the financial figures of the athletic department. Perhaps more important, he assured Crisler that Fielding Yost, the former Michigan coach who was then athletic director, would not interfere with his coaching.

That was a sticking point for Crisler, who had heard of Yost's heavy-handed ways with the coaches who had followed him after his retirement. For his part, Yost was not a Crisler-backer. He wanted to hire Tom Hamilton, the coach at Navy.

Yost, and many of the Michigan alums, also didn't care for the idea of hiring a Chicago man, considering the rich rivalry between the two schools.

1933
Princeton coach

It had been Stagg's team in 1905 that broke the Wolverines' 56-game unbeaten streak.

In mid-January 1938, Crisler wrote Aigler informing him he was withdrawing his name from consideration.

Aigler again requested a meeting in New York. Crisler laid out his demands — a free hand to coach the team as he saw fit without interference from Yost; selection of his own assistants; a promise that he would be named athletic director when Yost retired in 1941, or earlier if Yost vacated the position; and the title of assistant athletic director until he became athletic director. He also asked for more money than any coach in the Midwest had made — an estimated $15,000.

"I thought my terms were so far out of line that they would be unacceptable," Crisler said later.

Crisler was surprised when Michigan offered the job on Feb. 8, 1938. The next day, he resigned from Princeton.

"Michigan presents such a far-reaching opportunity that it was difficult for me to do anything but accept," Crisler wrote in a letter to Princeton officials after taking the Michigan job.

Crisler had his work cut out for him at Michigan, which was exactly the way he liked it. He inherited a program from Kipke that had seen both highs and lows. Kipke started coaching at Michigan in 1930 and proceeded to lead the Wolverines to four straight conference titles, including national

Crisler addresses his team in 1935. Princeton was voted national champions following a 9-0 record.

championships in 1932 and 1933. But Michigan began to slump through the next four seasons, and by the time Crisler arrived for the 1938 season, the administration and fans were restless.

As always, there was considerable correspondence between Stagg and Crisler during this time of transition.

"I shall not be disappointed, Fritz, if you don't win more than half of the games," Stagg wrote to Crisler, shortly after he took the Michigan job.

Two weeks later, Crisler spelled out the poor shape of the program he inherited.

"There is no doubt about it, Michigan is in a terrible mess, bad as the one that existed at Minnesota and Princeton," Crisler wrote to Stagg. "It will mean about two years of missionary work, which will involve a lot of speaking engagements."

Crisler completed the letter by saying, "I hope it will be my last move."

As he had done so well before when introduced at Minnesota and then at Princeton, Crisler turned on the charm at Michigan. He was introduced to the Michigan student body, which had a peculiar response to the new coach.

"Take it off, take it off," the students chanted.

Crisler removed his coat.

"Roll 'em up, roll 'em up," they shouted in unison.

Crisler rolled up his sleeves and trousers. Then he knocked them out. "Thank you," he said. "That was the first time I ever had to undress to make an address."

His timing was perfect, as was evidenced in his good fortune to be arriving at Michigan when Tom Harmon and Forest Evashevski were about to enter their sophomore years.

But before Crisler took the practice field for the first time that fall, he began to make considerable cosmetic changes. He brought with him from Princeton the tear-away jerseys he had created after losing a game when an opposing player grabbed his halfback by the sleeve.

Crisler then went about making a superficial change in equipment that today distinguishes Michigan football players from all others.

The Michigan helmets had been solid black, and Crisler wanted to give them distinction and make them useful at the same time. Crisler knew he was going to run the single-wing, noted for its speed and deception, and he wanted to make it as easy as possible for the players. At the time, most teams used dark, solid uniforms. To help passers spot their receivers downfield, Crisler had the helmets painted in their now distinctive maize-and-blue winged pattern, the maize highlighting the original stitching of the leather helmets.

Crisler was not one to reveal much about himself in letters or speeches, but it became increasingly obvious Michigan had one superstitious coach. While he was a player at Chicago, Crisler had found a penny on the field in 1920. He put it in his shoe that day, and for every game as a player or coach, Crisler had that penny in his shoe. He also had a lucky tie, suit and socks, and on game days, he and his coaches would drive the exact route down the same side streets every Saturday to Michigan Stadium.

He was a complex man who, superstitions aside, did considerable soul-searching. He used his psychology major and applied it to himself. He understood his weaknesses as far as football was concerned and immediately hired a coaching staff — Campbell Dickson, Earl Martineau, Clarence (Biggie) Munn, Bennie Oosterbaan and Walter (Wally) Weber — that could complement and improve his knowledge of the game. Oosterbaan had been a three-sport athlete at Michigan and was considered one of the finest athletes to have played there. Weber was U-M's freshman coach, and Munn, who was an all-America at Minnesota, would eventually become head coach at Michigan State.

Crisler brought equipment innovations and a new coaching staff to Michigan, but what he had waiting there for him was a gift, and that was Harmon.

Harmon Leads the Way

Crisler had few problems with his first team. Immediately he knew he had landed a solid group, but although he could detail practices, Crisler could never have plotted the career Harmon would have and the impact he would make at Michigan. Yost had considered Harmon, raised in Gary, Ind., the best high school athlete in the country. In Crisler's single-wing offense, Harmon would thrive, although his greatest moments were saved for his junior and senior seasons.

Harmon's primary blocker was Evashevski, his classmate and quarterback, who was a light-hearted young man with a mischievous streak. He would call his coach "Chris Fisler" and often teased Crisler. In one pre-game speech, Crisler told the team he wanted "11 tigers on defense and 11 lions on offense." Evashevski, who later coached at Iowa, raised his hand and said he would not play unless he could be a leopard.

1937
Last days at Princeton

Michigan athletic director Fielding Yost welcomes Crisler as the Wolverines new coach in February 1938.

Crisler shares his coaching philosophy with Yost (middle) and his assistants Wally Weber, Bennie Oosterbaan and Roy Courtright after arriving at Ann Arbor in 1938.

In Crisler's first season at Michigan, the Wolverines went 6-1-1 and finished second in the Big Ten. The Wolverines defeated Michigan State (14-0), which it had not done during the four previous seasons. Clearly, this team was a sign of things to come. Michigan outscored its opponents, 131-40, that year, a positive step considering Kipke's last team had been outscored, 110-54. The season was highlighted by victories over Crisler's alma mater, Chicago (45-7), and Michigan had shutouts in three of its last four games, including upsets of Illinois (14-0) and Ohio State (18-0) at Columbus, which prevented the Buckeyes from winning the conference title.

Harmon was not the Wolverines' main ball-carrier that season, but he rushed 77 times and averaged five yards a carry, and he completed 21 of 45 passes for 310 yards.

The key to Michigan's tricky, deceptive single-wing attack, that featured the fullback spinner, reverses and trap blocking, was Harmon in his final two seasons. He was a triple-back threat who could run, pass and punt, and he did them all equally well. In 1939, an injury to Paul Kromer forced Crisler to switch Harmon to left halfback. That season, he gained 884 yards on 130 carries, and he passed for 583 yards, helping Michigan finish 6-2.

Harmon was a machine, but Crisler's complex but well-rehearsed game plan kept his star and the rest of the team going. The players, some of whom found their coach to be stern and aloof, had little problem with the results he produced from their

Dr. Ralph Aigler (left), *a law professor at Michigan and the faculty athletic representative, recruited Crisler to become the Wolverines' new coach in 1938.*

tough, daily two-hour workouts. They found they were playing for an intuitive, innovative coach who lived for football.

"He'd tell us to watch for this to develop and be ready when that would happen," Harmon later wrote. "We'd be amazed when the things he predicted turned out as if it'd been rehearsed. He just knew football. He was such a student of it."

Harmon would later say the best team for which he played was the 1940 squad that finished 7-1 and ranked third nationally. Harmon never had the opportunity to play in a Rose Bowl, but he did get to play on the West Coast when Michigan met California at the Golden Bears' Memorial Stadium in the 1940 opener.

Michigan was one of the first teams to fly across the country for a game, chartering three United Airlines DC-3's for the two-day, three-stop trek to California. So serious was Crisler about this game, that once the team arrived, he sequestered them in a monastery for three days. Silence turned out to be golden as far as Harmon was concerned, because he was brilliant, accounting for four touchdowns in the Wolverines' 41-0 rout.

Harmon took the opening kickoff 95 yards for a touchdown, he returned a punt 70 yards for a score and rushed 86 yards from scrimmage, and avoided the attempt of a spectator trying to tackle him for another touchdown. He finished with 354 yards rushing on 29 carries.

A scout keeping tabs on Michigan for a rival wrote extensively about Harmon in his notes, emphasizing the halfback's ability in all phases of the game.

"Whatever you read or hear about Harmon can-

1938
With Son

not be exaggeration," the scout wrote. "Under no circumstances should the ball be punted to Harmon."

The scout was equally impressed by Crisler's team.

"Never saw a team that had their fundamentals, timing and faking perfected so soon in a season," he wrote. "They played like a bunch of professionals."

Michigan continued to play that way, winning the next four games, before traveling to Minnesota for a matchup of two of the best teams in college football. Michigan, captained by Evashevski, was ranked third, and the Gophers, which had won the last four league titles and three straight national championships, were ranked second.

So tightly contested was the game, the only scoring occurred in the second quarter. Michigan scored on a 2-yard pass from Harmon to Evashevski, but Harmon missed the extra point. Minnesota won the game, 7-6, thanks to halfback Bruce Smith, who ran 80 yards for the score.

For the remarkable personal success Harmon enjoyed, he was never part of a team that defeated the powerful Gophers, and he never scored against them. Harmon blamed himself for the loss in 1940. Early in the game, he slipped on Minnesota's 1-yard line and failed to score.

Two weeks after the loss to Minnesota, Michigan was on the road to Ohio State, and although it was one of Harmon's more memorable games, he remembered with amusement the trip from Ann Arbor to Columbus, and how this loose, jovial group finally got under their coach's skin.

"Crisler thought football players should be thinking about one thing all the time — football,"

Crisler poses with his son, Scotty, and wife, Dorothy, after their arrival in Ann Arbor in 1938.

Harmon told The Miami Herald in 1979. "On the way to the Ohio State game, everybody was talking about everything but football, mostly about the dates they had lined up after the game. This incensed Crisler.

"When the train got off at Toledo, he pulled everyone off and took us all to a hotel. He found a room to fit us all in, slammed the door and read us the riot act. We got back on the train, and as Crisler walked by, one of the players was talking about a date he had. Fritz got so mad, he went into his state room and slammed the door and stayed there the rest of the trip."

The players may have been loose on the train, but they meant business when they arrived at Ohio Stadium. In Harmon's final game, he scored three touchdowns, threw for two more and kicked four extra points in a 40-0 victory, the Buckeyes' worst loss in 35 years.

During his career, Harmon always was dominating against Ohio State. He missed only three minutes in three Ohio State games and scored five touchdowns, threw for four touchdowns and kicked seven extra points. Perhaps relieved to see him finally leave the college ranks, the Ohio State fans gave Harmon a standing ovation. It was a fitting send-off for a player who two weeks before had made the cover of *Life* magazine.

The career of "Old 98" was over, and his jersey was retired when he graduated. In three seasons, Harmon rushed for 2,134 yards, passed for 1,304, kicked 33 extra points and two field goals. Fittingly,

Harmon, whom most had considered the best ball-carrier since Red Grange, was awarded the Heisman Trophy.

"I am certain that were it not for Fritz, this halfback would never have gained the honors that came my way during my three years at Michigan," Harmon said years later.

Crisler kept a favorite picture of Harmon standing in the rain on the field at Minnesota, his sleeves ripped off and a large section of his shirt torn out. Harmon and the tear-away jersey went hand in hand, considering he went through 20 jerseys his junior year. During one game, an opponent, trying to tackle Harmon, got a handful of his jersey numbers instead. After the game, he sought Harmon and had him autograph the keepsake.

"The only thing I ever did for Tom Harmon was make sure he had a football to run with," Crisler said later.

Harmon might have brought national attention to Michigan, but after Crisler's third season as the Wolverines' coach, it was clear who was in charge and the architect of the game plan that made Harmon's success possible.

Early in his coaching career, including those first few years at Michigan, Crisler had a habit of playing hunches, which often backfired. He brought with him from Princeton, not only tear-away jerseys, but his tear-jerking, lengthy pre-game speeches. Crisler, though, always was willing to learn, and he learned from his mistakes.

By the start of the new decade, Harmon's final year, Crisler was becoming increasingly confident

**1940
Harmon on the
cover of *Life***

and polished. He dropped the emotionally draining pep talks and replaced them with rousing speeches, which he often delivered at midweek.

"He was a great motivator, but he wasn't the rough, gruff type," said Bump Elliott, who played under Crisler in the late 1940's and later coached at Michigan when Crisler was athletic director. "He could be very stern, but there was always a reason for that. Fritz didn't demand respect, he gained respect."

Another MacArthur

In that sense, he began to resemble the great military leaders he had so often read about and admired. George Trevor, a writer for The New York Sun, described Crisler in that way: "Both in appearance and in his flair for the dramatic he suggests General Douglas MacArthur."

Even his players recognized Crisler's highly disciplined, military qualities.

"I feel certain that had Crisler followed a military career, he would have been another MacArthur or Eisenhower," said Alvin Wistert, who played at Michigan from 1947-49. "He was extremely intelligent, tough as nails, thorough, and when he finished a pep talk, there was no holding back the team."

In a military training setting, drilling and routine are the norm. At Michigan, under Crisler, it was no different. His routine might have become just that, but what Crisler preached each day seemed to take hold. He had favorite phrases that he would use constantly. "Offense is poise," he would say, "Defense is frenzy". To bolster his players' confidence, Crisler used this pet phrase: "Our

Crisler's Dream Backfield of 1939: Forest Evashevski, Bob Westfall, Tom Harmon and Fred Trosko.

plan is simple. Theirs is one of desperation."

Crisler's favorite halftime ploy was used whether the team was winning overwhelmingly or losing. "What's the score?" he would ask the players. "Nothing to nothing," they would shout, even if they were annihilating their opponent. It was the response Crisler demanded and received time and again. By his third season at Michigan, he had perfected playing the mind games that would motivate the players.

"It was the last scrimmage in 1942 and Tom Kuzma ran a play and hurt his knee," said Don Lund, who played under Crisler from 1942 to 1944 and later coached the Michigan baseball team to

a national championship in 1960. "He was wincing in pain. Crisler walked over to him and said, 'Move your body, or move the team.' That got your attention. It was great motivation, because it let everyone know we weren't going to live or die with the big star."

Nothing seemed to get by Crisler. No flaw was too small for him to notice.

"I was playing left tackle, and the play went opposite me around right end," said Wistert, the last of three Wistert brothers to distinguish himself at Michigan. "My assignment was to make a check block at the line of scrimmage, then get to the cut-off. I didn't make the check block, and then

To Fritz —
In sincere appreciation for all
you have done — my best wishes always
to not only the greatest coach in the
world but also the greatest guy — Ol' "98"
will take you as the All American coach
every day —
Sincerely
Tom —

Harmon, a two-time all-America halfback in 1939 and 1940, won the Heisman and Maxwell trophies in 1940.

Crisler and his star halfback Tom Harmon, hold up the remains of his tattered jersey after his brilliant performance against Ohio State in 1940.

I heard Fritz yelling, 'Wisty, what are you doing?' And I thought, 'What the hell is he doing watching me?' The play was going around right end — he should be watching who's throwing the key block."

Crisler's players, as well as his colleagues recognized his ability not only to motivate, but to painstakingly plan an attack and have his players respond accordingly. Former Wolverine players who were coached by Crisler remember giving him more effort and sweat than they believed they were ever capable of giving.

Michigan was a national contender again under Crisler, and after three straight appearances in the Top 20, including a final ranking of third after the 1940 season, people were taking note of Crisler's abilities.

"No one could utilize the available talent like Crisler," said an unidentified rival coach. "Players sometimes said they didn't like him, because he was stern, aloof and driven. But they would die for him on the football field. He made them winners and respected individuals."

Said a former colleague: "He's a cold, calculating fish with a good reason for everything he does. It's a wonder he ever makes any mistakes at all."

There was no question who was in charge when Crisler took the field with his team. The players found him tough, but fair, and they called him either "Coach Crisler" or "Mr. Crisler".

"That wasn't because of anything he told us to do," said Bob Chappuis, who starred on the 1947

Forest Evashevski (right) was the emotional leader on Crisler's 1938, 1939 and 1940 teams.

team, and still finds it difficult to refer to his old coach as "Fritz."

"That's just the way it was."

Crisler was a strict disciplinarian who played by the rules and wanted no unsportsmanlike conduct from his players. Lund remembered his coach once telling the team, "There's no rule saying you can't block as hard as you want, tackle as much as you like. But remember that you're Michigan men — none of the extras."

His disciplined hand not only applied to his team, but to himself and the coaching staff. The staff met often and for long hours, going over game plans and devising new uses of the single wing. So detailed were his practice plans, written by hand with each line alternating in blue and red pencil, he literally plotted every moment leading up to the game.

"I believed in self-discipline," Crisler told The Michigan Daily in 1968. "A man should want to make his contribution as part of a unit, a team. I never really said it, but I made it pretty plain that a player who didn't agree with me on these things wouldn't be welcome on my squad."

He also did not welcome swearing on or off the field, which was something he picked up from his mentor, Stagg. After his second season at Michigan, Crisler wrote to Stagg and recalled how his old coach chewed out a teammate for cursing on the field.

"Since that day I have never uttered an oath on the field or will I ever," Crisler wrote. "I heard you once suggest to an assistant coach that abusive language directed at a player was rather a futile way to urge him to do his best."

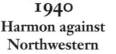

**1940
Harmon against
Northwestern**

Crisler always was seeking the best from his players, but he wanted to teach them along the way. Even 50 years later, the fact Crisler never belittled his players by swearing at them remains etched in their fond memories of the coach.

"He never used any profanity," Lund said. "About as far as he went was saying, 'Jackass.' If it was 'Double jackass,' you were really in trouble. Usually, he just had to look at you."

Crisler had the look of a winner, and he had the mind-set of one, too. He also had a new job in 1941. Yost had retired as athletic director, and Crisler eased into the position, as had been dictated by his contract.

Rebuilding after Harmon

He was about to enter his fourth season as coach, and he was faced with the challenge of maintaining Michigan's national prominence without its most nationally recognized player, Harmon.

"I know that many will take exception to this next statement, but I firmly believe that from a coaching standpoint, the revitalizing and reshaping of the 1941 team was possibly Crisler's finest hour," said Bob Westfall, who gained 688 yards and scored seven touchdowns that season, in a story that appeared in a U-M program.

Michigan opened the 1941 season with four straight victories, including shutouts against Iowa and Pittsburgh, before playing Minnesota in Ann Arbor. Bernie Bierman was entering his 10th and final season with the Gophers, who had earned six Big Ten titles and five national championships under his guidance.

Minnesota was ranked third nationally when the teams met, and for the fourth straight time, Michi-

An intense Crisler watches his Wolverines from the bench in 1941. U-M finished the season, 6-1-1.

gan lost, 7-0. If Crisler could find anything remotely amusing about Minnesota's dominance of the Wolverines, it was the fact that when Crisler left Minnesota, he had hand-picked Bierman as his successor.

"Little did I suspect that act would haunt me in later years," Crisler said in a 1968 interview.

The Wolverines shut out Illinois and Columbia, then tied Ohio State, 20-20, at Michigan Stadium. Michigan finished the season ranked fifth and tied for second in the Big Ten.

A year later, the nation was gripped by World War II, and Crisler and Aigler were sent to Washington, D.C., to promote the cause of college football and the need for its continuation during this difficult time.

In 1942, Minnesota, under first-year coach Dr. George Hauser, continued to give Crisler fits. The Gophers upset the fourth-ranked Wolverines, 16-14. Minnesota was a league rival, after all, and as is the case today, winning conference games is the coach's main goal. The Gophers' success gnawed at Crisler, but controversy was brewing with Michigan's nonconference rival, Notre Dame. Crisler, of course, was in the middle of it.

Battling the Irish

He was not thrilled Michigan was to resume its series with Notre Dame in 1942 after a 33-year hiatus. When the University of Chicago decided to drop its football program at the end of 1939, that left the Wolverines with open dates the next three seasons. That was just the opening Yost, still operating as athletic director in 1939, was hoping for. He wanted Notre Dame on the schedule, and

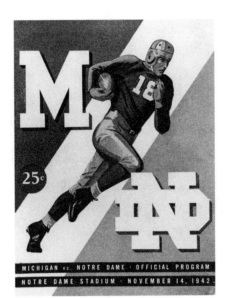

**1942
Game program**

Notre Dame wanted Michigan.

Crisler, though, wanted an Eastern school, like Pitt. By the end of May 1940, Yost and Crisler struck a compromise. Michigan would play Pitt in 1941 at Michigan Stadium, but would face Notre Dame in South Bend, Ind., in 1942, and would then play host to the Fighting Irish in 1943.

Crisler and Notre Dame's second-year coach, Frank Leahy, were completely different, but each shared a common goal — to push their players to perfection and, of course, to win along the way. Crisler was a Methodist and had early in his life considered a career in the ministry. Leahy was a staunch Catholic. Crisler was an innovator and used his creative mind to devise deceptive plays in his offensive-minded game plan. Leahy took what already was in use and improved on it. Stanford coach Clark Shaughnessy had revived the T-formation in 1940, and Leahy borrowed from that when he took over at Notre Dame.

The 1942 game took place during the tense, early months of World War II. More than 57,000 attended the game at Notre Dame Stadium, remarkable considering the restrictions on wartime travel and the fact neither team had an unblemished record. It was still Notre Dame-Michigan, and it was a diversion from the daily news of the war overseas. The game was carried on NBC radio and it was broadcast worldwide on the Armed Forces Network. Notre Dame (5-1-1) was ranked fourth nationally; the Wolverines (5-2) were ranked sixth.

"The game had been ballyhooed no end ever since it was scheduled and of course tickets were at a premium and scalpers demanding outlandish prices," Crisler wrote to Stagg several months after the game.

Michigan was coming off consecutive victories over Illinois and Harvard. So great was the pressure, Crisler refused reporters access to his practices.

Notre Dame's only loss was to Georgia Tech, which had been ranked second nationally. So intense was the pressure on Leahy to beat Michigan, he reportedly took his team to the grave of legendary Notre Dame coach Knute Rockne a few hours before the game.

The Fighting Irish were having problems adjusting to the T-formation, which was led by Angelo Bertelli at starting quarterback, but they scored first on a pass play. Notre Dame moved through the air, but Michigan took to the ground, going 53 yards — all rushes — to tie the game at 7. The Irish got a boost just before halftime, recovering a Michigan fumble at the Wolverines' 12. Notre Dame scored to make it 14-13.

"Crisler asked me to tell the players about Notre Dame during the half," said Kip Taylor, one of Crisler's scouts and a former Michigan player who was the first to score a touchdown at Michigan Stadium. "I said they have three weaknesses, and I spelled them out, and they went out and hammered those weaknesses to beat them."

Michigan made defensive adjustments at halftime and specifically focused on Notre Dame's weakness at tackle. The Wolverines took the kickoff to open the third quarter and literally had a field day, scoring three touchdowns in the first eight minutes for a 32-14 lead. Two of those scores were set up by Michigan-forced Notre Dame turnovers, a fumble on a kickoff and an interception of Bertelli.

**1942
Crisler and his
lucky Chevy**

Michigan won, 32-20, and in Michigan fashion, the Wolverines controlled the clock, running 78 plays — 69 rushing — and gained 319 yards on the ground.

The Notre Dame renewal was of huge interest, but no game mattered more league-wise than the next one, Michigan-Ohio State. Michigan was ranked fourth nationally after defeating Notre Dame. But what happened to the Wolverines after that game gave fuel to Crisler's argument that playing the Fighting Irish was detrimental to Michigan's goal of winning league games.

It had rained in Columbus, from early that morning through the game, and the wet conditions forced Michigan to eliminate some of its intricate ball-handling. The Buckeyes won, 21-7, and Crisler wrote later that the Wolverines probably would have lost that game regardless of the weather. Not only was Ohio State a good team — they were ranked fifth and went on to win the conference and national titles — but the Notre Dame game had drained the Michigan players.

"Our kids left practically everything on the field at South Bend and didn't have any sharpness at Columbus," Crisler wrote to Stagg two months later.

Michigan won its final game over Iowa to finish 7-3 overall, 3-2 in the Big Ten, and was ranked ninth in the final poll. In Crisler's letter to Stagg, he discussed the 1942 season in detail. It was clear the victory over Notre Dame made a season in which Michigan finished in a third-place tie in the conference, tolerable, if not enjoyable.

"The Notre Dame game, of course, was a great victory for all Michigan people," Crisler wrote in

From left to right: 1942 U-M captain George Ceithaml, assistant Bennie Oosterbaan and Al Wistert pose with Crisler and his lucky Chevy for a promotional photo.

his letter to Stagg on Jan. 11, 1943. "Our kids were all hopped up and played the best game of the season. The score could have been more in our favor but I am very happy that it was not.

"They (Notre Dame) had collected such a crowd of football stars that everybody thought they were invincible. That pressure began to pile up in the summer and the coaching staff began to press. They had the team at South Bend practicing most of the summer and after classes started they worked from 5 to 7 in the morning and from 3 to 6 in the afternoon. The Notre Dame kids began to feel the pressure and the results of overcoaching."

By 1943, the face of college football was changed by the war, and Crisler remarked at the time that

peace-time coaching was different than what college coaches endured during wartime.

Many of the schools around the country lost players because of the war effort — several schools like Alabama, Tennessee and Boston College dropped their programs — but many benefitted from military officer training programs based on their campuses. In the Midwest, Michigan, Notre Dame, Purdue and Northwestern were sites of these military programs. An Ohio State player, for example, assigned to Northwestern for officer training, could continue to play football, but he would do so at Northwestern. Michigan's starting center in 1943 was Fred Negus, who was Wisconsin's center in 1942. Elroy (Crazy Legs) Hirsch and Bill

Crisler with Elroy Hirsch (far left) and Bill Daly, Jack Wink and Paul White after a 1943 preseason practice.

Daley were assigned by the Marine Corps to Michigan.

The Wolverines were dominating the first three games, beating their opponents by a combined score of 104-13. Next up was Notre Dame at Michigan Stadium.

The teams were almost completely different from the previous year. Notre Dame returned only two starters from the 1942 team, including Bertelli, and Michigan had three starters back. The teams met the second weekend in October with Notre Dame (2-0) ranked No. 1 and Michigan (3-0) ranked No. 2. Crisler was aware of the revenge factor at Notre Dame.

"Last year the Notre Dame kids played as fine and clean football as any team we played," Crisler wrote to Stagg on Nov. 8, 1943. "They, of course, were greatly disappointed and have been smarting under their defeat for a year. This year they threw everything at us with holding and all the extras. They made a religious crusade by issuing religious bulletins and of course they had their team pitched very high."

Crisler was not one to make excuses, but Michigan had seven backs injured, and the offense did not click. Bertelli, who went on to win the Heisman Trophy that year, was impeccable as he led the Notre Dame offense. The Irish sent a man in motion on nearly every play, and Michigan did not have the defense to cover properly. Notre Dame led, 21-6, at halftime, and eventually defeated Michigan, 35-12. During that season, no other team was able to score more than seven points against Michigan. Notre Dame finished the season undefeated and won the national championship.

"I think we probably were at our worst against Notre Dame," Crisler wrote to Stagg. "Everything worked for them and it was one of those days for us."

Crisler made his team get back to work for the game against Minnesota two weeks later. The Wolverines rebounded in astounding fashion, annihilating the Gophers, 49-6, to regain the coveted Little Brown Jug.

That was just the start for the Wolverines, who rolled through their next four opponents, hold them to a combined 19 points. Crisler would earn his first Big Ten championship and the Wolverines were ranked third, equaling their best finish under Crisler.

1952
With Bob Hope

Michigan had fulfilled its obligation to the two-game series with Notre Dame, and Crisler wanted no more of it. Leahy asked to renew the series, but Crisler would not budge.

Wrote Ed Fitzgerald in *Sport* in November 1943: "There is absolutely no question that a feud of sizable proportion is raging between (Frank) Leahy and Fritz Crisler. Neither misses an opportunity to slam the other, even if in genteel terms, and hardly a month goes by that new coals aren't heaped on the fire of disagreement."

It is clear from Crisler's correspondance with Stagg and others that he did not think highly of Notre Dame, although he never said as much publicly. On April 10, 1944, Crisler wrote to Stagg about the leveling off of college football because the experienced players who had been in the officer training programs would be sent overseas. From what he had learned, though, Crisler speculated Notre Dame would not lose a step because of its connections nationwide.

"For your information only, they have access to the lists of men to be assigned at colleges and coaches check the names that they would like to have on this list and get everybody they ask for," Crisler wrote. "This, of course, comes from high up in Washington and I am told it is Postmaster General Walker, who is a Notre Dame graduate.

"Notre Dame just had assigned to them the 22 best football players from the State of New York. The worst feature about this is that such practices may get back to some of the authorities in the Navy and they may feel inclined to discontinue the whole athletic program among the Navy and Marine trainees in the colleges."

In private correspondance, Crisler often questioned the integrity of Notre Dame, and that might have been a source of his disinterest in playing the Irish. Crisler was a play-by-the-rules coach and an NCAA rules committee member who eventually became its chairman.

Coaches not always are great fans of each other, but Crisler admitted in an interview with The Detroit Times in 1948, his first year as a retired coach, he never knew what to think of Leahy.

"I don't know why I don't like Frank Leahy," Crisler was quoted. "I don't know why I do like Frank Leahy. He's a total enigma. One morning you see him and he's full of fun, full of life. The next morning you see him, he's morose and gloomy. One day you think he's going to fight fair. The next day he's telling you how he's going to destroy you. Some say his teams play rough but don't play dirty. I'm never sure what Leahy thinks is the difference between rough and dirty. I just don't know what to make of the man."

Crisler never game himself the chance to coach again against Leahy. After the 1943 game, Crisler remained adamant in his refusal to schedule Notre Dame for two reasons. He honestly believed if the series with Notre Dame was resumed, it would split the loyalty of the Michigan fans. His thinking was that Michigan fans who were Catholic might be persuaded for religious reasons to back Notre Dame. His other reason, the one he emphasized publicly, was that conference play was Michigan's focus, and a game the stature of Michigan-Notre Dame would take away from that focus.

That is a belief Bo Schembechler, who later coached the Wolverines and never favored adding Notre Dame to the schedule, maintains to this day.

"No game can be more important than a conference game, especially Ohio State," Schembechler said in an interview. "I always agreed with him (Crisler) on that."

There are not many letters in Crisler's personal files like the one he wrote to Stagg concerning what he thought was Notre Dame's unfair advantage with the officers assigned there for training. One interesting find was the copy of the letter Crisler wrote in confidence to Big Ten Conference commissioner John Griffith in March 1944. He asked Griffith to destroy the letter, but Crisler filed his copy.

"I have been a bit disturbed about Notre Dame being identified so closely with the conference in recent meetings," Crisler wrote. "Their representatives haven't contributed much, and I do know that they use this association in promoting the idea that Notre Dame conforms entirely with Conference regulations. So far as the public is concerned, I think it is felt that they have the blessing of the Conference in whatever they do. I do happen to know that they are not going along all the way with the Conference."

It is more than evident from that letter that Crisler resented Notre Dame. And even more clear was the fact Crisler would have nothing to do with Notre Dame, especially on the football field.

In the fall of 1946, Crisler was fully in control not only of Michigan's football team but the athletic department, as well. He also was in control of the Michigan-Notre Dame destiny, which as far as he was concerned, had no future. He backed an official policy that year that somewhat defined Michigan's scheduling process and eliminated Notre Dame from the mix.

It would be by conference rule that of Michigan's nine regular-season games, only three could be against nonconference opponents. Since Michigan State was not a conference member, the Spartans accounted for one of the three games. One game would be against an Eastern school and the other against one from the West.

Crisler now had Notre Dame where he wanted — off his schedule. He could not, though, rid himself of Notre Dame entirely.

By the early 1950's, Crisler was deeply involved with the NCAA rules committee, and that position carried with it tremendous power. In 1952, the NCAA rules committee publicly admonished Leahy for an illegal shift employed in a 9-0 victory over Southern California. A year later, Leahy was chided again for giving summer tryouts to athletes being considered for scholarships.

Although Leahy endured public criticism for both incidents, his career suffered considerable damage later in 1953 when Crisler was chairman of the NCAA rules committee. Following a game with Iowa that ended in a 14-14 tie, Leahy admitted he twice had a player fake injury so that the clock would stop, giving Notre Dame time to set up their touchdowns. Notre Dame knowingly had cheated, and Crisler suggested that subject would be discussed at the next rules committee meeting.

Crisler and assistant Bennie Oosterbaan visit prior to a Big Ten meeting in Chicago in 1944.

In the boxes containing some of Crisler's scrapbooks and correspondances, there also are several folders of "squawk" mail. Those letters usually were from Michigan fans who didn't like plays he called during the years he was coaching, and after he retired from coaching, they turned to what was wrong with the current football team and athletic department.

Some of the most interesting items were sent by Leahy's brother, Gene, who took the opportunity to write Crisler twice.

"Had IOWA profited by (the faked injuries), nothing would ever come of it," Gene Leahy wrote.

"That and the so-called sucker shift become a CRIME only when Notre Dame uses them. ... Why don't all of you, Mr. Crisler, who hate to see Notre Dame win, make a New Year's resolution to be FAIR WITH NOTRE DAME, in the interests of true sportsmanship."

Crisler replied to Gene Leahy's letter and also sent a copy of the reply to Frank Leahy.

"When you make the charge that I am anti-Notre Dame and that I am one who hates to see Notre Dame win, your indictment is so unfair and slanted that I even hesitate to make any response to your letter," Crisler wrote.

Crisler also wrote that he never questioned Frank Leahy's ethics because he never saw the USC or Iowa games. He added that the subject of the faked injuries would come up in the January 1954 meeting of the rules committee, but he would not be the one raising the issue.

After that meeting, the NCAA made it publicly known that it considered Leahy's faked-injury ploy dishonest and unsportsmanlike, although the committee took no action against the coach. Leahy, though, was ill and, encouraged by his doctors, retired that January.

Gene Leahy sent one final, stinging letter to Crisler.

"I KNEW you could do it, as you did a year ago, point the finger of accusation at Notre Dame," Leahy wrote. "If you had a spark of sportsmanship in you, Mr. Crisler, you would schedule Notre Dame, and try to beat them LEGITIMATELY on the gridiron, rather that with subterfuge worthy of Russia's Molotov. HE don't care who he maligns just so it is THE UNITED STATES, and YOU don't care who YOU malign just so it is NOTRE DAME.

"YOU have not had the GUTS to play Notre Dame since 1943 when they humiliated your DREAM TEAM, and have resorted to every foul trick within your reach to discredit them ever since.

"If YOU are a shining example of sportsmanship and lily-white ethics in sports, then STALIN should have become POPE."

Two years after he coached his last game against Notre Dame, Crisler did not have the Irish on his mind. The nonconference openings on Michigan's schedule were filled by Michigan State, Army and

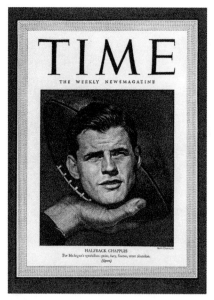

1947
Chappuis on the
cover of *Time*

Navy, and he had other items of importance that concerned him.

As Crisler had anticipated, wartime had affected college football, and in 1944, the conference decided to relax its rule concerning freshmen and allowed them to play with the varsity. The Wolverines were coming off an 8-2 record in 1944, in which they had finished the season ranked eighth. Crisler entered the 1945 season with a young team.

The Two-Platoon System vs. Army

The Wolverines were loaded with inexperienced 17-year-olds, and they faced the unenviable task of playing a loaded Army team in the fifth game of the season. Michigan, with six freshmen starting, was 3-1 and ranked ninth going into the meeting with top-ranked Army on Oct. 12 at Yankee Stadium.

Michigan was expected to be no match for the Earl (Red) Blaik-coached Cadets, led by Felix (Doc) Blanchard and Glenn Davis. The Cadets had the advantage of fielding a team of 23-year-olds who had already served their time overseas. They were bigger, stronger and more experienced.

Crisler recognized Michigan's odds of beating Army were not good, but he also recognized a loophole in the substitution rule that had been changed in 1941 in anticipation of the effect the war would have on the game. The rule allowed a player in the game "at any time" instead of once a quarter.

"Those three little words changed the game," Crisler later said.

It was out of necessity that Crisler developed two-platoon football — dividing the team into offensive and defensive specialists — and he drilled the Michigan team in this new style of play for two weeks before the Army game.

"I knew we couldn't stay on the same field with Army man-to-man, but the rules had been liberalized during the war so coaches could substitute freely with as many men as they wanted to," Crisler told The Michigan Daily in 1968. "It suddenly occurred to me that if we could use any boy whenever we wanted, why not look for the best ball-carriers, passers and receivers and put the best blockers up front ahead of them, then take them out when the ball changed hands and throw in the best tacklers and pass defenders."

The 70,000-plus in attendance had to be surprised not only by Crisler's ingenuity, but that it seemed to actually be working against the highly acclaimed Cadets. The teams were scoreless in the first quarter, a moral victory for Michigan. Blanchard, who would gain 179 yards against the Wolverines that day, scored on a 69-yard run to give Army a 14-0 halftime lead.

Michigan, which remained fresh and active because of the platooning, came out in the third quarter and drove 75 yards in 11 plays for its first score to make it 14-7. Army scored the game's final points, a pair of touchdowns in the third and fourth quarters, but the game will be remembered for Crisler's brilliant maneuvering.

"It was no ingenuity on my part but desperation," Crisler said later. "When the other fellow has a thousand dollars and you have a dime, it's time to gamble. Our below-par wartime squad couldn't possibly have stood up against that powerhouse for 60 minutes. Therefore, we gambled.

"Many coaches wrote and phoned to know what

1948
Rose Bowl program
═══════════════

we were doing. By the following season, many of the colleges and high schools had begun to adopt platooning."

Two-platoon football made the T-formation popular, because the quarterback could specialize on offense. Crisler, though, maintained his allegiance to the single wing. Dividing teams into offensive and defensive units was not for everyone, though. Crisler's innovation had its critics, and one publication went so far as to call it "push-button" football, because it took the thinking out of football.

Ironically, in 1953 — when Crisler was head of the NCAA rules committee — he was a major force behind outlawing the unlimited substitution rule, which had allowed him to create two-platoon football. To have the best players make up offensive and defensive units, coaches around the country began to realize they needed more players and they had to recruit young men who specialized in those positions.

Crisler, who always believed the reputation of the school was enough to get student-athletes to attend, was an opponent of the way the recruiting process was evolving. He did not believe in coaches hitting the road to sell their programs. By eliminating the unlimited substitution rule, the number of players needed would diminish, as would the need for recruiting.

Army and Michigan would meet again in 1946, this time in the third week of the season. The second-ranked Cadets still had two of the nation's best halfbacks in Davis and Blanchard, who would go on to win the Heisman that year, but the Wolverines were ranked fourth and seemed to have a fighting chance.

"Let's quit ... you'll never get it done right," Crisler told the team, ending the practice. It was the same ploy Stagg had used with the young Crisler so many years before. And as it had worked then with Crisler, it worked with this Michigan team. The next day, the players pleaded with their coach for another chance. They got it, and they were unstoppable from that moment on.

New York Gov. Thomas E. Dewey, a Michigan alumnus, presents Crisler with the Coach of the Year Award in January 1948 in New York City.

Nearly 86,000 jammed Michigan Stadium, and they saw one of the greatest games in Michigan history. Halfback Bob Chappuis led the Wolverines to their first score on a 12-yard touchdown pass to Howard Yerges with 11 minutes left in the first quarter. Davis tied the score with 50 seconds left in the quarter. Army led, 13-7, at halftime, but Michigan opened the second half with an 83-yard scoring drive to tie the game.

Blanchard scored the game's final touchdown to give Army a 20-13 victory, but Michigan's defense stifled the Cadets' two great runners. Blanchard had 14 carries for 44 yards and Davis gained 64 yards on 17 attempts. The Cadets were stunned by Michigan's offense, which equaled their first downs — 12 — and nearly matched them in rushing yards. Michigan gained 141 yards on the ground, Army 152.

1951
As U-M
Athletic Director

The Wolverines' performance in that game had so captured the nation, Chappuis was featured on the cover of *Time* magazine in 1947. Michigan finished the season ranked sixth with a 6-2-1 record, 5-1-1 and second place in the Big Ten.

A Season to Remember

In his decade of coaching at Michigan, Crisler will be forever known and remembered for his undefeated 1947 team. Crisler, a Civil War buff who visited the major battlefields four times, was ready for his final tour, and he had an attack that was challenged only twice that season.

Chappuis recalled the main problem Crisler faced before that season began. World War II had ended, and there was an interesting mix of young players and those who had returned from military

duty a bit older, wiser and maybe even a little jaded.

"Some of those fellows were sort of blase, because we had been over there and seen so much already," Chappuis said.

Chappuis enrolled at Michigan in 1941, but enlisted the following year after he had played some in 1942. He flew B-25 bomber missions into Italy and was shot down on his 21st mission and spent three months with the Italian underground. He returned to Michigan in 1946. Elliott was another whose college years were broken up by the war. He had enlisted in the Marine Corps reserves in high school and was called up in 1943 when he was sent to Purdue for officer training. At Purdue, Elliott played football, basketball and baseball. He was commissioned to second lieutenant and spent 10 months in China. He, too, returned to Michigan in 1946.

Crisler's other challenge was the size of his team. Michigan was small, the largest player weighing 220 pounds, and the offensive line averaged only 182 pounds. Much of the nation was enthralled by the T-formation, but Crisler was at his imaginative best in the single wing. Size did not matter much in that offense. It was about skill, quickness and ball-handling, and this team had it all.

In Michigan's backfield was Howard Yerges at quarterback, Elliott and Chappuis at halfback, and Jack Weisenburger at fullback. Dick Rifenburg and Bob Mann were the ends, Don Tomasi and Joe Soboleski the guards, Bruce Hilkene and Bill Pritula the tackles, and J.T. White was the center.

The Wolverines' playbook consisted of 170 plays, and they used combinations of double-reverses, buck-reverse laterals, criss-crosses, quick hits and spins from seven different formations.

"It was fun to play that system," Chappuis said in an interview. "We had one play where the fullback took the ball from center and handed it to the upback who pitched it to me. I handed it to (Bump) Elliott, and he handed it to the end, who threw it to the other end. The ball was touched by seven people! After the Rose Bowl, the students had the film of the game and were showing it in Hill Auditorium. They asked us to narrate the film. Half the time we didn't know who was handling the ball, and we'd end up using the wrong names. And often, the camera would miss the play."

**1956
Touchdown Club
Award Honors**

If Crisler could help it that season, no one would miss an assignment and no play would be bungled. He was 48 and in his 18th season as a head coach. His knowledge of the game was equaled only by his ability to motivate his players. Practices would not end until he witnessed perfection.

"We did rehearse until he was satisfied, until we knew what we were doing and how to do it," Chappuis said. "If he would see one thing that didn't fit the picture, he would make us continue to work until we got it right."

One day during practice that season, it was a particularly rough day and things weren't going right.

"Let's quit ... you'll never get it done right," Crisler told the team, ending the practice.

It was the same ploy Stagg had used with the young Crisler so many years before. And as it had worked then with Crisler, it worked with this Michigan team. The next day, the players pleaded with their coach for another chance. They got it, and they were unstoppable from that moment on.

Crisler's assistant, Oosterbaan, was the relaxed coach, the one who would have fun with the players. Crisler, perhaps disappointed by the 1946 season after finishing second in the conference and losing out on a chance to go to the Rose Bowl, was fixated on perfection.

It was this team that dubbed their coach "The Lord," although Crisler never heard his players refer to him that way.

"We'd sit there and say, 'Do you think it will rain for the game?' And we'd say, 'Well, The Lord wouldn't allow it,'" Chappuis said. "He was very austere. You could never feel like you could get very close to him. He was interested in you as a football player, but other than that, he was standoffish."

As Harmon had related years after his career at Michigan, Crisler wanted his players to think of nothing but football when they were preparing for a game. Certainly, Crisler's psychology degree was useful in coaching. Even now, his former players heap praise on Crisler for his ability to motivate. Wistert, a two-time all-America who played on the 1947 team and was Michigan's captain in 1949, once said that after Crisler finished a pep talk, there was no holding back the team.

"My estimation of Fritz is he expected professional performances from amateurs," Wistert said. "You have to demand excellence from kids or you don't get it. Fritz demanded so much of you as a player. He was no-nonsense."

But that was the key to Crisler. Not only was he always prepared, but he was always watching,

Crisler is flanked by the two coaches who succeeded him at Michigan: Bump Elliott (left), who led the Wolverines from 1959 to 1968, and Bennie Oosterbaan, who coached from 1948 to 1958.

A prototype goal post which Crisler designed to be on the goal line. It was used during the 1950's and 1960's.

always learning and always figuring out the best ways to work his players.

"I don't know anything about coaching, but I've heard enough about it, and most will tell you coaching is getting people in the right frame of mind," Chappuis said. "That's a real trick, and he was so good at it. He was magnificent at it.

"He got more out of me than I thought I had in me. From my point of view, I never felt I had a great deal of individual talent. He just knew how to get the best out of me."

Apparently, Crisler was able to get the best from everyone in 1947. The Wolverines destroyed Michigan State, 55-0, in the opener behind three touchdowns from Chappuis. Against Stanford in the second game, Michigan scored four touchdowns in the first eight minutes and rolled to a 49-13 victory. Going into the game against Pittsburgh, Michigan was

ranked second. The Wolverines blitzed Pitt, 69-0, and earned the nation's top ranking.

Even during this run, Crisler never took anything for granted, particularly when conference play began. The Wolverines had little problem against Northwestern, winning 49-21, although they gave up the most points they would allow all year.

"We knew we had some good football players and we felt we should do well," Crisler told The Ann Arbor News in 1979. "But we didn't know what was going to happen when we went out on the field. That's where the games are won, so we had to be prepared. I always said that your biggest game is the next game on the schedule."

The Wolverines' next two games were their biggest. Minnesota took an early 6-0 lead, but Chappuis completed a 40-yard pass to Elliott for the tying touchdown, and Jim Brieske kicked the

A trio of legends: Harmon (left) and Oosterbaan (right) join Crisler at a 1977 U-M-Ohio State game.

extra point to give Michigan the lead. A touchdown by Gene Derricotte in the second half gave the Wolverines the advantage for good, and they went on to win, 13-6. They dropped a spot in the national rankings, though, and Notre Dame became the No. 1 team.

The national press was so awed by Crisler's team that was so deftly deceptive, the Wolverines were called the "Mad Magicians." Ninety-percent of the plays Crisler devised had at least one exchange, and frequently as many as three.

"We had to handle the ball so much and as they said, so magically," Chappuis said. "We loved to amaze people with our agility."

Crisler never admitted this during the season, but he later would say his 1947 team even amazed him.

"They could even fool the coaches closely observing the plays they themselves had made up," Crisler said later.

During the week of the Illinois game, Crisler decided to make a change in the blocking on punt returns. He switched blocking assignments from the wide side to the short side of the field. In the first quarter against the Illini, the move worked. Elliott took a punt on the Michigan 26 and ran to his left, the wide side. He then cut back and ran up the right sideline for a 74-yard touchdown return. Illinois tied the game at 7, but Hank Fonde scored to give Michigan a 13-6 victory.

"As a player, you never went into a game where you didn't think you were better prepared," said Elliott, Michigan's only two-way player that season, in an interview. "We believed that, and it was true — we were better prepared. That was one of the keys to his (Crisler's) success, the great preparation."

Even as the Wolverines continued to roll through their schedule, Crisler would not let up. Nothing would sway his focus.

"If anyone during the season said something like, 'Oh, boy, we're one step closer to the Rose Bowl,' that was the end," Chappuis said. "You sat down the next game."

In their final four games, the Wolverines never gave an inch, outscoring their opponents, 145-6. The final two games of that span were at Wisconsin and at home against Ohio State. It had been snowing hard in Madison, Wis., and the field had to be shoveled so the game could be played.

"It was still snowing that day, and Fritz told Yerges we weren't going to use any of our razzle-dazzle plays," Wistert recalled. "Hell, we used every play in the book."

Michigan rolled over the Badgers, 40-6, and the Wolverines came home and defeated Ohio State, 21-6, to clinch a perfect regular season and a trip to the Rose Bowl. Michigan finished the season leading the nation in total offense, averaging 413 yards, and in passing with a 174-yard average.

**1965
at Rose Bowl**

The "Mad Magicians" gained publicity because of their offense, but Elliott and Wistert emphasized that Crisler was a great defensive mind. Besides Elliott, Wistert and Derricotte, Michigan's defense featured Len Ford, Dan Dworsky, Quentin Sickels and Dick Kempthorn.

"He would get the scouting report, and Fritz would go over it, telling us, 'Before they go across midfield, they're apt to do so and so,'" Wistert said. "The offensive plays would unfold just as he said they would. It was amazing. I would think, 'My God, they're doing what he said they would.'"

Before the OSU game, Michigan had regained the No. 1 ranking, but the Wolverines were moved down a spot after shutting out Ohio State, because Notre Dame had destroyed Tulane, 59-6.

Although Michigan and Notre Dame were not playing each other at the time, they were embroiled in yet another controversy. The Associated Press writers' poll was taken at the end of the regular season, and the national champion was determined at that point. Notre Dame did not participate in bowl games at the time.

As the Irish headed into their final game on Dec. 8 against Southern Cal, they had the No. 1 ranking — barely. They had only a four-point advantage over Michigan in the voting. Notre Dame traveled to Los Angeles and thumped USC, 38-7. In the final AP poll taken after that game, the Irish won hands-down, earning 107 first-place votes to Michigan's 25.

Individual honors also were awarded after the regular season. Chappuis, who led the conference in total offense for the second straight year, was named all-America and finished second in Heisman Trophy voting behind Notre Dame's Johnny Lujack. Elliott was named the conference and Michigan's most valuable player, and he, too, made all-America. Crisler beat out Notre Dame's Frank Leahy for coach-of-the-year honors.

Awards aside, the Wolverines still had something to prove. They had to play USC in the Rose Bowl, and finally put to rest the burning question of the day — Which was the better team, Michigan or Notre Dame? USC was a common opponent, one of three Notre Dame and U-M shared.

(The others were Pittsburgh and Northwestern. Notre Dame defeated Pitt, 40-6, and Northwestern, 26-19).

The Wolverines took the train to Los Angeles, a 33-hour trip. They entered the game as 14-point favorites, but Crisler would not let the team get caught up in prognostications. In fact, he was as hard on them as ever.

Crisler watches a Michigan game from the press box following his retirement in 1968.

"We were running through our plays, and I pulled a hamstring," Chappuis said. "I was lying on the ground, and our trainer, Jim Hunt, was looking at me. Coach Crisler came over and asked what happened. Jim said, 'It looks like he pulled a hamstring.' Crisler responded, 'Good thing it didn't happen to somebody who could run.' He knew how to motivate me. He was a genius. I couldn't wait to get up and run."

Naturally, Crisler had done his homework on Southern Cal. He even used his former player, Tom Harmon, who was then playing professionally in Los Angeles, as a scout. Harmon watched Southern Cal, in person, play six times and dutifully took notes for Crisler.

"He wanted to know everything, even which way the seams of the ball were turned when it was snapped," Harmon later told The Miami Herald. "He had so many plays you wouldn't believe it. He had six or seven new plays for every game that he used only once. He didn't use half his offense against Southern Cal, otherwise, the score would have been 102-0."

Crisler was prepared, as usual, and he made certain that despite the time change, the Wolverines would be ready for the afternoon game.

"Preparing a team for a big game is a delicate thing," he told The Los Angeles Times several years later. "The team I brought here in 1947 reached its peak at exactly 2 p.m., the exact time the game started."

So exact was Crisler's game plan, he had assumed Southern Cal would try to find a way to put handcuffs on Michigan's deceptive offense. He made changes of his own to throw off the Trojans.

"We put in a formation in which all the linemen were on the one side of the center except one guard," Crisler said in a 1979 interview.

"We used a shift in the line. We hadn't shown that before, and I thought it would confuse them a bit.

"We used it right at the start, and they lined up like it was a regular play in the usual positions, with as many men on the weak side as the strong side. We scored two touchdowns in the first half, set up by running to the strong side. After we scored the second touchdown, I told the players not to use the formation again unless we got in trouble."

Michigan never was in trouble, completing its perfect season with a 49-0 victory. They broke nine Rose Bowl records and finished with 491 yards of total offense; the Trojans could muster only 133. Chappuis threw for 188 yards and two touchdowns, and he rushed 13 times for 91 yards. Weisenburger, who also rushed for 91 yards, scored three touchdowns, each on 1-yard runs.

"We did have a bunch of wonderful guys," Chappuis said. "We all got along well and still do. It was a perfect season in every way."

"It was a fun season," Elliott recalled. "It really was one of those years everything clicked."

Even Crisler could enjoy the moment, and he often would share a humorous tale of the moments following the Rose Bowl.

"One of the most amusing things about that game was what happened after the game as I was walking into the dressing room," Crisler said in a 1979 interview with The Ann Arbor News. "This young fella, he was from Michigan, came up and said, 'We have to do something about the coaching.' I said, 'What's wrong. We won the game, didn't we?'

"He said, 'Well, in 1902 we played Stanford and won, 49-0. Look what happened today. We play USC and we win, 49-0. We haven't improved a damn bit in 46 years.'"

Perhaps the most amusing and intriguing thing that happened to the players after that game occurred during the long train ride home. The players had taken over the observation car, and they were allowed beer.

"We were having a party," Wistert said, laughing as he recalled that evening. "Each guy was supposed to tell a story or a joke. Halfway through the evening, Fritz poked his head in the car and said, 'Can I join you?' Joe Soboleski said to him, 'As long as you can supply the booze and tell a story as good as the last one.' Fritz laughed and said, 'OK, I can do that.'

"I remember we all thought it was odd."

The Wolverines handled Southern Cal so impressively, The Associated Press, in an unprecedented move, conducted another poll. Writers nationally were asked to pick either Michigan (10-0) or Notre Dame (9-0) No. 1.

Results of the second

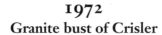

1972
Granite bust of Crisler

Crisler's coaching record

Year	Team	W	L	T
1930	Minnesota	3	4	1
1931	Minnesota	7	3	0
1932	Princeton	2	2	3
1933	Princeton	9	0	0
1934	Princeton	7	1	0
1935	Princeton	9	0	0
1936	Princeton	4	2	2
1937	Princeton	4	4	0
1938	Michigan	6	1	1
1939	Michigan	6	2	0
1940	Michigan	7	1	0
1941	Michigan	6	1	1
1942	Michigan	7	3	0
1943	Michigan	8	1	0
1944	Michigan	8	2	0
1945	Michigan	7	3	0
1946	Michigan	6	2	1
1947	Michigan	10	0	0
Total		**116**	**32**	**9**

Fritz Crisler's teams won 3 national championships – in 1933, 1935 and 1947.

AP poll were revealed Jan. 6, and Michigan won with 226 first-place votes; Notre Dame finished with 119. Media guides from Michigan and Notre Dame indicate both claim the 1947 national championship. The Michigan players were awarded national title rings to prove it.

"I know we were as good as Notre Dame," Elliott said.

That Michigan team has met to commemorate the 1947 season several times, the most notable its 25th anniversary in 1972. Crisler was quite ill and had been hospitalized, but he made it to the reunion. He did not talk that night. Instead, he wrote each player a sentimental, emotional letter that most of them framed. It was the first time their old coach had shared his emotions, the first time he seemed so human.

"There are times when the heart is too full for utterance. Being with you on the 25th anniversary was one of those times," Crisler wrote.

He told the players about life travels and how the cheers they heard all those years ago as Michigan players might fade, but the friendships created then would never cease.

BO SCHEMBECHLER

By Chris McCosky

Return to Glory

"We must have started with 150 guys when he came here," said Jim Betts, a backup quarterback in 1969. "After that spring, we were down to 75 or 80. A lot of players resented Bo because he was so damn demanding. But it was a strong group who stayed." It was that group which laid the foundation for Michigan's return to prominence.

It all began like a scene straight out of a Frank Merriwell or Horatio Alger story.

An unknown football coach who had known great success at a small college in Ohio is tapped to become the head football coach at one of the most storied football powers in college football history, the University of Michigan.

On an early January morning in 1969, he and his youthful staff of six eager assistants load up in a small caravan of cars and head north on a seven-hour drive through the farmlands of Ohio with dreams of conquering Big Ten opponents, winning the Rose Bowl and the fancy newspaper headlines that would follow.

But then came a problem. After arriving in Ann Arbor and driving around for 15 or 20 minutes, the new head coach and his staff of assistants can't find the college.

Finally, the lead car in the entourage pulls into a nearby hotel parking lot. The new head coach gets out, heads inside to the lobby, finds a pay phone, and calls the Michigan football office.

"Yeah, hi, this is Bo Schembechler, the new football coach. Where are you?"

A humbling beginning for a new head coach who had much to prove? Perhaps.

But Schembechler and his staff would quickly find the road to glory for the Michigan football program.

And for the next 21 seasons it would be an unforgettable run.

Yet on Dec. 26, 1968, the selection of Schembechler as Michigan's football coach was a choice from left field.

Schembechler had built a powerhouse at Miami of Ohio in six seasons with a 40-17-3 record and a pair of Mid-American Conference titles. However, he wasn't the big-name coach such as a Darrell Royal or a Joe Paterno whom the Michigan

Bo Schembechler was a star pitcher for Barberton High in the mid-1940's.

alumni were clamoring for. Still, he was the choice of Michigan's new athletic director, Don Canham.

Schembechler had been brought to Michigan under a stealthy setting nearly ten days earlier, on Christmas Eve 1968, by Canham to replace the popular Bump Elliott, who had coached at Michigan for 10 seasons and had taken the Maize & Blue to the Rose Bowl in 1965, and was now retiring after an 8-2 season to move into a newly created associate athletic director's position, where he would be assisting Canham.

Oddly, it was Elliott who had placed the first call to Schembechler to discuss with him the possibility of taking the Michigan job. Elliott would later meet Schembechler on a cold, gray snowy morning at the Detroit airport when he arrived for his visit on Christmas Eve and bring him to the offices at 1000 South State Street to meet with Canham, who was waiting for them in his office. The university campus was mostly deserted during the holiday break and all of the athletic department employees had been given the day off. It was the perfect time to be sneaking a prospective new coach in for a visit.

The trio of Canham, Elliott and Schembechler would huddle for nearly half a day. They talked of where the Michigan football program was, where it had been and, most importantly, where it needed to go.

1950
a Miami (Ohio) tackle

Schembechler then laid down the rules if he was to come: He had to be able to coach the team his way. And he had to have his people.

Realizing that a bond of mutual respect and trust between the Wolverines' athletic director and the prospective new coach had been built, Canham made Schembechler the offer of becoming Michigan's next coach. He would inherit the legacy that Yost, Kipke, Crisler and Oosterbaan had built before him.

Without pausing to think about it or touring the campus and its athletic facilities, Schembechler accepted the offer.

There would be no written contract, just a handshake between Canham and his new football coach. Schembechler's salary would be $21,000 — a mere $1,000 raise over the amount he was receiving from Miami.

Schembechler would later recall this memorable point in time.

"They didn't have to sell me on anything or show me the campus," Schembechler said. "I knew why I was here — the opportunity.

"As for the money — I would have come for less."

Two days later, the new Michigan football coach would return to Ann Arbor to meet the university's Athletic Board. He was registered at the local Hilton Hotel under the somewhat fictional name of Glenn Schems.

A day later, on Dec. 27, Schembechler faced the Ann Arbor and Detroit media for the first time. They couldn't spell his name correctly and most couldn't pronounce it.

But when he spoke he got their attention.

"I came here to win — and win now," Schembechler stated with confidence and determination.

"And we're gonna win my way."

Bo Arrives

Schembechler's arrival in Ann Arbor with a crew cut and a conservative coaching style would prove to be a culture shock for many.

"Remember now, this was 1969," he would explain later. "The Vietnam conflict was in full force and there were anti-war demonstrations everywhere. The students had taken over the president's office. There was racial tension, there was long hair, there was rock music and psychedelic drugs.

"And there was me. A small-town guy with small-town values. A short-haired guy who believed in discipline and hard work."

Of course, everybody told him that his paramilitary approach wouldn't work in liberal Ann Arbor. To which he replied: "If it don't, then I won't be here long because I can't do this any other way."

The Michigan program was in a deep sleep when Schembechler arrived. The once-proud Wolverines had won just one Big Ten title in the previous 18 years. They had had five losing seasons in the previous 10 years and their 100,000-plus seat stadium was averaging barely 70,000 fans a game.

And the facilities were awful. The coaches, after a long day's work during preseason practice, used to sleep in the clubhouse of the campus golf course.

1954
at Presbyterian

Their dressing room was at Yost Field House and their "lockers" were nothing more than nails in the walls.

"Men," Schembechler told his staff, "we are going to make a few changes here."

The first thing he did was to facilitate a program-wide, university-wide attitude adjustment.

"When I got there, the rub on Michigan was that they were talented but not very tough," he said. "I vowed that nobody would ever say my team wasn't tough. They may say we were a no-talent team or that we had the dumbest offense and defense in the country, but they would never say we weren't tough."

On the first day of spring practice, Schembechler lined up his players and delivered the first of many legendary speeches:

"Now you listen to me. All of you. I do not care if you are white or black or Irish or Italian or Catholic or Jewish or liberal or conservative. From this point on, I will treat you all exactly the same — like dogs!"

And he did. He put those unsuspecting players through the most hellish spring of their lives. Double sessions every day. Weight-room work and extra running afterward. Extra running on Sundays. Schembechler was all over them every step of the way, yelling, grabbing face masks, throwing them around, slapping them with yard sticks, demanding that they give more, demanding that they get tougher.

"You know what," Schembechler said later, "that was exactly what they were looking for. Oh, they hated me. You bet your ass they hated me. But when they saw the results, they felt so much better about themselves and they accepted it."

Somewhere in the middle of that spring, as players were quitting left and right, Schembechler came up with the slogan, "Those Who Stay Will Be Champions," and hung it above the locker room.

"We must have started with 150 guys when he came here," said Jim Betts, a backup quarterback in 1969. "After that spring, we were down to 75 or 80. A lot of players resented Bo because he was so damn demanding. But it was a strong group who stayed."

It was that group which laid the foundation and paved the way for Michigan's return to prominence in college football.

"We lived up to that slogan," Schembechler said.

Wars with Woody

That first season was like one long, gradual crescendo of emotion —

As an assistant at Ohio State, Bo clowns around with his prize linemen, Darryl Sanders (76) and Bob Vogel (73), prior to practice.

starting slowly, almost haltingly, with early losses to Missouri and Michigan State, but building like a tidal wave with lopsided victories over Minnesota, Wisconsin, Illinois and Iowa. The apex came against Ohio State in the last game of the regular season.

"You have to understand that when we came to Michigan, we set one goal and that was to beat Ohio State," Schembechler said. "Everything we did was done with that goal in mind. The Buck-

eyes were the most dominant team in the Big Ten and in the country. Nobody could beat them. We designed our defense to stop their power running game. We designed our offense to be just like theirs so our defense could practice stopping it. Ohio State was our obsession. I figured if we wanted to beat them so badly, our hunger would carry us through the first nine games."

Schembechler's obsession with Ohio State had a personal angle. Schembechler had played for Ohio State coach Woody Hayes at Miami in 1949 and 1950, and was his assistant coach at Ohio State in 1951, and from 1958-62. Just about everything he knew about football and coaching he learned from Hayes.

In fact, Hayes tried to discourage Schembechler from taking the Miami job in 1963 by telling him, "Bo, you are going to be the next head coach at Ohio State."

Schembechler's comments to the media on the eve of his first game against Ohio State in 1969 illustrated his emotion for the battle: "I am about to fight my football father."

The crescendo had reached deafening levels by that Saturday in November. The Wolverines, who were 17-point underdogs, had begun chanting, "Beat the Bucks, Beat the Bucks," in the locker room after their victory in Iowa the previous week, and they hadn't let up.

When Schembechler led his team onto the Michigan Stadium playing field for pre-game warm-ups, he saw Hayes and the Buckeyes already out there warming up, on Michigan's side of the field.

"We hadn't even hit the field and he had already attacked me," Schembechler said.

Hayes was testing the mettle of his protégé and the move backfired. Schembechler sent his troops out to where the Buckeyes were, walked up to Hayes and said, "Coach, you are warming up on the wrong side of the field."

Hayes, his tactic trumped, grumbled and motioned his players to the other side of the field. The Michigan players went ballistic. They had just seen their first-year coach send the master marching downfield.

Back in the locker room before the game, Schembechler had only to say two words to ignite his highly combustible team: "It's time."

Indeed, it was time.

Upstart Michigan shocked the sports world that day and won the Big Ten title by whipping the Buckeyes, 24-12, a victory that at the time was labeled as one of the biggest upsets in college football history.

Schembechler later explained: "It put our program on the map. I mean, Schembechler wasn't exactly a household name in those days.

During a 6-year period from 1963-68, Bo's Miami of Ohio teams achieved a 40-17-3 record and won 2 Mid-America Conference titles.

"But put it in perspective. We were playing a team that was considered one of the greatest college football teams of all-time. They had won the national championship the year before and had won 22 straight games. It was the best team Woody Hayes ever coached. And we destroyed them. The great Buckeye offense had committed seven turnovers and we ran over that great defense for 24 points. I mean, that was a special game, a magnificent upset."

Schembechler said the crowning moment for him was a letter he received from legendary Michigan coach Fritz Crisler, who had watched the game from his hospital bed.

"He said how proud he was that day to be a Michigan man," Schembechler said. "How proud he was of the way Michigan stood out that day and once again expressed its dominance in college football."

And those who stayed were champions. Twelve of the next 20 Michigan teams won Big Ten titles. No Big Ten team won more football games in the 1970's than Michigan. From 1969-78, Michigan and Ohio State would battle on the final day of the season to determine the Big Ten champion — Bo won five times, Woody won four times and once there was a tie.

"Those games were everything I lived for," Schembechler wrote in his book, *Bo: Life, Laughs and Lessons of a College Football Legend*. "Lose and

U-M athletic director Don Canham (middle) announces Bo's hiring as the Wolverines' new football coach on Dec. 27, 1968 to replace the retiring Bump Elliott (right).

your world was gray. Win and you were in heaven. Last game of the season. Buckeyes against Wolverines. Woody against me. Maybe it was a personal thing. Maybe it was just two proud teams. But it was the best of rivalries."

The Early Years

He was born in Barberton, Ohio, a small town near Canton on April 1, 1929.

It was his sister, Marge, who gave him his famous nickname. As a baby, she tried to say "brother," but she could only say "Bobo ... Bobo."

The nickname stuck and he's been "Bo" ever since.

As a youngster, Schembechler's life was a series of ballgames. He played them all, but dreamed of being a major-league player.

As a teen-ager, he followed Notre Dame football and hoped to earn a college scholarship to play for Frank Leahy.

On autumn Saturdays, he listened to the radio, keeping up with the exploits of Angelo Bertelli,

On the sideline during his first game as U-M coach, Bo savors a 42-14 victory over Vanderbilt in 1969.

A rare moment: Bo relaxes in his office prior to the Texas A&M game in 1970.

Creighton Miller, Johnny Lujack and George Connor.

Schembechler starred as a 5-foot-10, 190-lb. tackle at Barberton High. Following his senior year, Schembechler's beloved Fighting Irish didn't offer him a college scholarship to play football, but Ohio State, Michigan and Miami of Ohio actively recruited him.

In the end, he opted to go to Miami to play for Sid Gillman.

Before Schembechler's junior season, Gillman left Miami to take the head coaching position at arch-rival Cincinnati. He also took half the team, including the Redskins' best quarterback, Gene Rossi, and halfback, Danny McKeever.

Gillman's replacement was a young coach from Denison named Woody Hayes, who quickly made his presence felt.

Hayes was a screamer who coached football much like George Patton ran the 7th Cavalry during World War II.

He was everywhere on the football field, challenging and belittling players and making life miserable for the entire squad.

Miami finished with a 5-4 record in 1949 with Schembechler starting at tackle.

In 1950, Woody's torturous training methods began to pay dividends; Miami finished 9-1, after trouncing Arizona State, 34-21, in the Salad Bowl on New Year's Day.

In one of the most memorable games in 1950, Miami met Cincinnati in the season finale on a snowy field. The contest looked more like an old intrasquad scrimmage with Rossi, McKeever & Co. facing their former teammates.

A popular rally cry among the Miami team that week was, "Let's show them what they left behind."

Schembechler played perhaps the best game of his college career as Miami won, 28-0.

In a newsletter to Miami recruits describing the game, Hayes wrote, "Bo Schembechler, our offensive tackle, draped the snow-covered field with

An intense student of the game, Bo and an assistant review films of an upcoming opponent.

Cincinnati defenders. ... "

Schembechler was on Cloud Nine afterward.

Following the 1950 season, Hayes was offered the head-coaching job at Ohio State. And after graduating from Miami, Schembechler joined him as a graduate assistant for one season.

The relationship between Schembechler and Hayes grew to be a close one.

"He affected me in every imaginable way — and some unimaginable. I swear I heard his voice in my sleep," Schembechler would later explain.

Hayes' 1951 Buckeyes were a mediocre team who would finish with a 4-3-2 record. In their final game of the season, Ohio State traveled to Michigan and lost, 7-0. The Buckeyes' offense lacked firepower. Vic Janowicz, who had won the Heisman Trophy a year earlier as a junior, yet hadn't made much of a contribution all season after Hayes had switched from the single wing to the T-formation, was unable to add much spark to the ailing Ohio State offense.

The day after the game, Hayes called his entire

Bo and all-America tackle Dan Dierdorf examine the special shoes that the Wolverines would wear on the new artificial turf at Michigan Stadium in 1969. U-M posted a 5-1 record on the new turf.

team and staff together for a meeting. With everyone assembled, a film projector was turned on and the game film from the Michigan contest came to life.

After 10 minutes, a frustrated Hayes got up, walked over, grabbed the projector and heaved it across the room with a crash.

He then served notice: "I will not subject the people of Columbus to that kind of football."

Hayes then walked out of the room, leaving behind a shocked audience.

The following summer, Schembechler was drafted by the Army. He would play service ball for two seasons.

In 1954, he began a decade of traveling, serving as an assistant coach at four different schools. His first stint was one-year assignment at Presbyterian College in Clinton, S.C., on Bill Crutchfield's staff.

Presbyterian won six games and lost three that season and Schembechler grew to love the slow

Five U-M great football coaches graced the front cover of the 1969 Michigan-Ohio State game program: (left to right) Harry Kipke, Fritz Crisler, Bennie Oosterbaan, Bump Elliott and Bo Schembechler.

pace and genteel Southern lifestyle.

The following year, he joined Doyt Perry's staff at Bowling Green and the Falcons posted a 7-1 record. Don Nehlen, the present-day coach at West Virginia, was the backup quarterback on that squad.

In 1956, Ara Parseghian left Miami of Ohio to go to Northwestern and offered Schembechler a spot on the staff. He would stay there for two seasons.

Northwestern went 0-9 in 1957. In their final game of the season, Illinois clobbered the Wildcats, 27-0, with Ray Nitschke breaking a 70-yard touchdown run that went in front of the North-

western bench.

It was a humiliating conclusion to a long season.

A few weeks later, Hayes would have an opening on his staff at Ohio State and offered it to Schembechler.

At first, Schembechler hesitated about taking the offer because he didn't want to desert Parseghian after a horrible season. But Parseghian and Wildcats assistant coach Alex Agasse — who both knew of Schembechler's loyalty — told him to take the offer, because it was too good of an opportunity. Their reasoning was solid. After the

Bo addresses reporters in the locker room after the Wolverines' 24-12 victory over Ohio State in 1969.

1957 season, Hayes' Buckeyes were ranked No. 1.

Schembechler's tenure with Ohio State would last five seasons. During this period, he would become Hayes' closest confidante, friend and heir apparent. The Buckeyes' record during this period was 30-11-4.

But during this glorious era at Ohio State, there is one dark moment which Schembechler will always remember. It occurred in 1961, after Ohio State has just whipped Michigan, 50-20, to wrap up the Big Ten championship and would be named national champions at season's end.

He and Hayes were in Cleveland for an alumni banquet at the Hollenden Hotel when Hayes got the word that Ohio State's Athletic Board of Control had voted to decline its invitation to the Rose Bowl. They determined that Ohio State's on-the-field success was beginning to jeopardize the school's academic standing. Minnesota would go to Pasadena instead.

Hayes exploded with rage. Eventually, after he and Schembechler took a long, silent walk through the streets of Cleveland, Hayes decided to go ahead and address the alumni gathering: "These people who have voted this decision today have never played in a Rose Bowl. They cannot comprehend the pride and the confidence and the lifelong memories that a game like this gives the young men who play college football. To deny those men this precious chance is the worst judgment they could possibly exercise."

It was the first time Schembechler had ever seen his mentor cry.

After the next season, in 1962, Johnny Pont left Miami of Ohio to take the head coaching job at Yale.

Suddenly, Schembechler's alma mater was looking for a new football coach.

After Schembechler was approached by several Miami of Ohio alumni, he went to Hayes to tell him he wanted the Miami job.

But Hayes had other plans. He quickly banged his fist on the desk in his office, responding, "You can't leave."

"What do you mean, I can't leave?" Schembechler asked.

"You can't leave," he said, "because you're going to be the next coach at Ohio State."

Schembechler then asked, "Woody, how much longer are you going to coach?"

"Three to five years. No longer," Hayes explained.

Schembechler, confident that Hayes would be staying at Ohio State much longer than he stated, decided to take the Miami job anyway.

"Gee, Woody," he said apologetically, "I'm ready to go now. I shouldn't wait around."

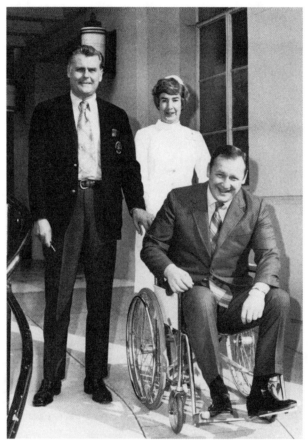

Bo leaves the hospital after a heart attack, which occurred prior to the 1970 Rose Bowl game.

Schembechler was right. Woody would remain at Ohio State for another 16 seasons.

Run-in with the Big Ten

In his first five seasons at Michigan, Bo Schembechler's Wolverines had amassed a record of 48 wins, six losses and one tie, had either won outright or tied for the Big Ten title four times and been to the Rose Bowl twice.

Life for the Maize & Blue couldn't have gotten any better. Yet, following Michigan's 10-10 tie in 1973, Schembechler suddenly found himself at odds with his Big Ten brethren.

The recent contest with Ohio State was one that gave definition to the term "smash-mouth" football. Michigan had two chances to win, but a pair of last-minute attempts by kicker Mike Lantry missed the mark.

Michigan and Ohio State would share the Big Ten title that season and, because the Buckeyes played in the Rose Bowl the year before, Michigan was expected to go to Pasadena.

"Boy, we're going to have great representation out there. Good luck, Bo," Hayes told Schembechler after the game.

But the next day, the Big Ten athletic directors, strong-armed by Commissioner Wayne Duke, voted to send Ohio State to the Rose Bowl. They

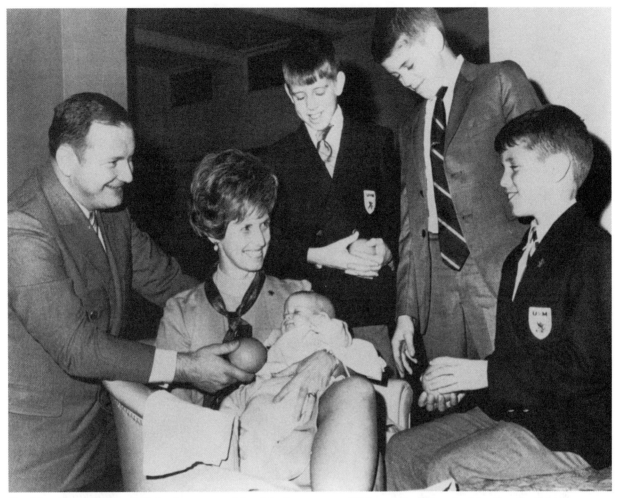

Bo, his wife, Millie, and their three sons visit with the newest addition to the Schembechler family, Schemy.

said that because Michigan's quarterback, Dennis Franklin, had been injured and would be unable to play in the game, and because the Big Ten had lost four straight Rose Bowls, Ohio State would a better representative of the Big Ten.

It was Schembechler's turn to rage.

He was in a Detroit television studio about to tape his weekly show when he got the news. The studio didn't stand a chance. Schembechler tore the place up and then proceeded to rip apart Duke and every athletic director in the conference.

"I want Wayne Duke to come before my team and tell them they aren't good enough," he told reporters. "I want him to tell Dennis Franklin that in his medical opinion he is not capable of playing against Southern Cal.

"I want him to look Larry Cipa (the backup quarterback) in the eye and tell him he's not good enough to quarterback Michigan in the Rose Bowl."

The quotes appeared in newspapers across the country and played a key role in changing the rules regarding the Big Ten's bowl representation.

Later, while he was telling his players they wouldn't be going to the Rose Bowl, Bo Schembechler broke down and cried.

Bo carried that bitterness toward Big Ten administrators the rest of his career.

"Let's face it," he would say later. "There were some very weak character guys in Big Ten athletic director positions. That's been proven. We had to get the determination of the Rose Bowl participants out of their hands. We were the better team

Bo discusses strategy at the chalkboard with tight end Jim Mandich prior to the 1969 Ohio State game.

and I know we would have beaten USC without Franklin. To deny that team a chance to play was criminal. And I vowed to never forget what happened. I told myself that if I ever let up on my bitterness over that decision, then I wouldn't be doing justice to those players."

However, there was some good that came of that heartbreak. As a result of the 1973 decision and Schembechler's unrelenting tirade, the Big Ten eventually overturned its antiquated rules prohibiting Big Ten teams from repeating in Rose Bowl games and from playing in other bowl games.

In 1975, Michigan became the first Big Ten team to play in a postseason bowl other than the Rose Bowl. They lost in the Orange Bowl to eventual national champion Oklahoma.

"As a result of what happened to us, we got the Big Ten to change those dumb rules, but it was a hell of a price," Schembechler said. "Our teams from 1972 to 1974 won 30 games, lost two and tied one. We outscored our opponents, 918-200, and had 11 shutouts. And those teams never played in a single bowl game. And today I hear teams complaining about playing in 'minor' bowls. Tell one of those guys from the 1973 team about minor bowls."

A Lesson Learned

The year is 1939. A 10-year-old Bo Schembechler, sitting idly in his living room in Barberton, Ohio, is jolted by the sound of his father cursing and slamming the phone down. He had never seen his mild-mannered father so angry.

Years later he would find out what had happened. His father, Shem, a fireman, was in line to be promoted to chief. It came down to him and another candidate and the results of a civil service exam would determine who got the job.

Shem's friends had called that night to tell him that the other candidate had obtained the answers to the exam. They offered to give him a copy of the answers.

"Never," Shem said.

He took the test clean. The other guy, who did cheat, beat him by a point and got the promotion.

Shem Schembechler walked up to the guy afterward and said, "You son of a bitch. I know how you got that score and I'm not working for you."

And he never did.

Bo Schembechler never forgot that story, nor the integrity of his old man.

More than 50 years later, in 1990, he, too, would be placed in a similar situation.

Schembechler, in his second year as athletic director at Michigan, received a call from Big Ten commissioner Jim Delaney telling him that he would soon be issuing a press release announcing that in 1993 Penn State would join the conference.

Schembechler was flabbergasted. It's the first he'd heard of this. Delaney had brought Penn State into the Big Ten without consulting the conference athletic directors. He had gone over their heads and dealt directly with the university presidents.

Schembechler, deeply insulted, confronted Michigan president James Duderstadt and, pulling no punches, promptly told him that he could never work for him again, that he couldn't trust him.

**1972
at Rose Bowl**

On Jan. 7, 1990, just a few days after his final game in the Rose bowl, Bo Schembechler resigned as athletic director.

Yes, like father, like son.

Woody is Fired

In the final days of December 1978, Bo Schembechler, choking back the tears, walked into his staff meeting with his coaches and told them: "The old man is gone. They fired the old man."

Woody Hayes. Fired by Ohio State. Schembechler knew it would happen one day, but it didn't lessen his remorse or his dismay.

Schembechler knew the minute he watched Hayes punch a Clemson middle guard during the Gator Bowl that his mentor's days were done.

"He went into seclusion for a while after that, but finally Doyt Perry and I convinced him to meet us at Doyt's place in Bowling Green," Schembechler said. "It was the dead of winter, and we were just sitting there going over all the old days. Suddenly, Hayes asks if we'll read a chapter of a book he's writing called *Let's Set the Record Straight*.

"I remember, I asked him what he meant by the title. He said, 'I think I ought to start out by clearing up that Gator Bowl thing.' And I asked him what he wrote."

Hayes' version of the incident floored Schembechler. Hayes started out by saying he had never seen a replay of the incident, but that he knows in his heart he did not hit the guy.

"Woody felt that the middle guard, who had intercepted the pass and was tackled on the Ohio State sideline, was taunting his players," Schembechler said. "Woody said that all he was trying to

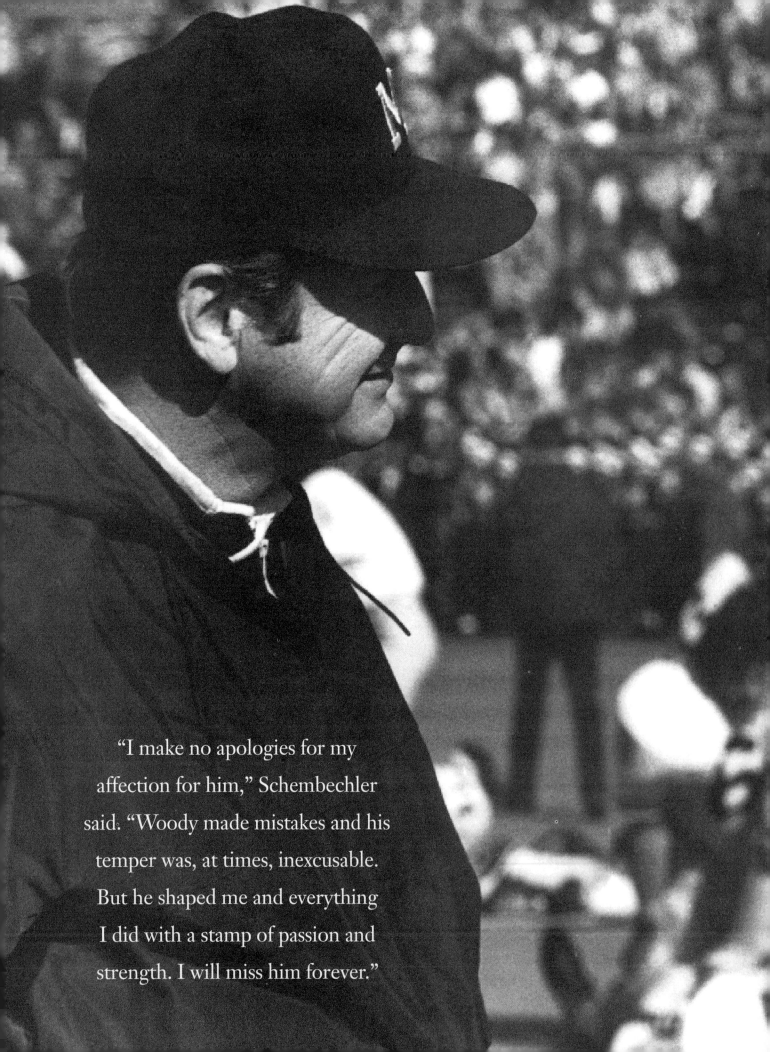

"I make no apologies for my affection for him," Schembechler said. "Woody made mistakes and his temper was, at times, inexcusable. But he shaped me and everything I did with a stamp of passion and strength. I will miss him forever."

Bo, on the sideline in 1971, prepares to send in a play in the Wolverines' 63-7 win over Iowa.

Bo celebrates Michigan's 22-0 victory over Ohio State in 1976 and a Rose Bowl selection.

A disgusted Bo on the sideline in the final moments of Michigan State's 24-15 upset of Michigan in 1978.

leave here tonight, we're going to have ourselves a deal." To which Schembechler replied: "No, we're not."

Still, after meeting with Texas A&M's president, Frank Vandiver, Schembechler hadn't turned down the offer. He said he wanted to take the offer back to Michigan and think it over.

Michigan athletic director Don Canham, somewhat begrudgingly, offered Schembechler a $25,000 raise to stay. Which brought his salary to $85,000 annually — and still $130,000 under the A&M offer.

"Maybe I am more appreciated elsewhere than I am here," Schembechler told his wife, Millie.

The news of Schembechler's possible departure eventually leaked out and reporters camped out around his house, waiting for him to make a decision.

Here, as he first recounted in his book, *Bo: Life, Laughs and Lessons of a College Football Legend*, is how the decision was reached:

" 'Millie, what do you think?' "

Bo enjoys a victory ride after Michigan defeated Ohio State, 14-6, in 1977.

bechler are worried. His team had just beaten Ohio State to clinch its second straight undisputed Big Ten championship and the old coach looked positively glum. He seemed distracted, preoccupied. Heartsick, even.

He was.

"It dawned on me as I was walking off that field that I had just coached my last game at Michigan Stadium," he said.

After 21 seasons, he had, at the constant urging of his family and doctors, decided to put away his whistle and yardsticks and retire from coaching.

But he didn't want the public or his team to know about it. Not yet. He told his staff. He told the administration. He had everything worked out so that the program, with Gary Moeller taking charge and a roster stocked with present and future all-Americas, even one future Heisman Trophy winner (Desmond Howard), wouldn't skip a beat.

He had scheduled a full team meeting for Dec. 13. It was then he would tell his players and then break the news to the public.

Unfortunately, the headlines of the Dec. 13th edition of The Ann Arbor News beat him to the punch: "Bo to Resign," screamed the bold print. Radio and television stations quickly picked up on the story and by the time Bo walked in to face his team, everybody knew why they were there.

"First of all," Schembechler told his team, "I want you to know how sorry I am that the news leaked out and you didn't hear this from me first. But it's time for me step aside. The Rose Bowl will

" 'What's in your heart, Bo?' "

" 'Mil, that's a lot of money. We'd be set for life.'

"She was crying. I started crying. I thought about the kids I had just recruited, how I promised them if they worked hard, by senior year, they could be starters. I looked around my basement, at the projectors and the clipboards and the football memorabilia.

" 'Millie,' I said, shaking my head, 'I just can't leave Michigan.'

" 'Then don't. We can get by on any amount of money.'

"She was right. The whole attraction was money, and that is no reason to take a job."

It was never about money for Schembechler. It was about loyalty. Loyalty to his family, his coaches, his players and his university.

"I'll never have a job I love as much as this one, and I knew it the first day I

Bo and one of his infamous yardsticks at a 1978 practice. Typically, if he only broke 3, it was a pretty good practice.

set foot on campus," Schembechler said. "Don Canham could have hired anybody in 1969 and they might have done as good or better than I did. But nobody would have ever had the respect for the job like I did. Nobody."

Mr. Off-Tackle

In 1971, Michigan was 11-0 in the regular season and threw exactly 114 passes, the fewest by a Michigan team in the modern era.

"That's where I got my reputation for '3 yards and a cloud of dust,' and 'Mr. Off-Tackle.' Truth is, we had to run all the time that year," Schembechler said. "Our quarterback, Tom Slade, was a great athlete

and good leader but he had a very average arm. We also had an unstoppable running attack with the great Billy Taylor and Glenn Doughty and an offensive line that included all-Americans Reggie McKenzie and Paul Seymour. So, what should we have done with that group?

"Do I like the run? Hell yes. But don't tell me I didn't utilize the pass. Don't tell me Rick Leach and Jim Harbaugh didn't pass the ball. Don't tell me Anthony Carter was wasted in our system. In 1988, with Michael Taylor and Demetrius Brown at quarterback, we averaged 153 yards passing a game and threw just two interceptions all year. Now, tell me about passing efficiency.

"But the simple truth in college football is, if you can't run the football, you aren't going to win. Take last year's (1995) championship game. Florida, in my judgment, has the greatest system of passing in the country. Nebraska — though they've built on it and changed it some over the years — still operates out of the basic premise that you line your big offensive linemen up and knock the other team off the line of scrimmage. You can have the greatest passing attack in the world, but there's still going to be third-down-and-short, and there's still going to be goal-line plays, and you had better be able to come off the ball and block and run. Nebraska beat Florida because the system at Nebraska is tougher."

Final Days at U-M

The year is 1989. Those close to Bo Schem-

be the last game I coach. But you listen to me and you listen to me good. We ain't turning this into some 'Win it for Bo' thing. Dammit, the Rose Bowl is your game. You earned it by winning the Big Ten championship. Now, we're going to go out there and we're going to win, but we aren't going to win for me. You got that?"

Quickly, though, the fire went out of his voice. He blinked hard and lowered his head.

"Men," he said. "The one thing I'm going to miss the most ... the one th ..."

Strangled by the lump of emotion pumping from his heart into his throat, the words stopped.

The players looked around in bewilderment. He's crying, they said, the old man is crying.

Derrick Walker, the team captain, said, "It was so damn strange. Nobody had ever seen him cry before. It was an incredibly moving moment."

As if to shake the words free, Schembechler began to pace across the long platform in front of the players.

"It was one of those paces where the heels hit hard and the thoughts hit just as hard," said all-American lineman Matt Elliott.

Eventually, he got back to the podium.

"The thing I will miss the most ... is my players."

Later, at his news conference, the same words would again become thick and stick in his throat.

"The toughest thing I ever had to do is give up my football team ... but ... I'm doing it."

If there were doubts as to why Schembechler coached, what pushed him at that crazy 16-hour, seven-days-a-week pace for 37 years, what made him devote his entire life to it, there's your answer.

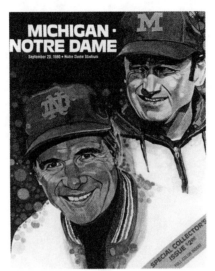

**1980
Game program**

It wasn't for money, for fame or for national championships. It was for the players.

And from the minute word of Schembechler's resignation got out, those players flooded the media with notes and quotes, tributes and testimonials, and their favorite Bo anecdotes.

"I think the fact that Bo is leaving just four wins short of Woody Hayes (among career Division I coaches) says something," Moeller said. "It shows that all these things he told kids about awards and records not being important was something he really believed."

All-American Greg Skrepenak added: "I'm not sad and I'm not disappointed. I will miss him, sure I will. But I know in my heart he will always be there for me, whether he's on the sideline or not."

Said Walker: "He teaches you character. He teaches you how to act, how to handle yourself in public situations. He teaches you to care about people and be concerned about things outside of football. He teaches you about life."

On and on, for days, the tributes continued. Perhaps none summed up Schembechler's impact better, though, than Dan Dierdorf, a member of Schembechler's first team and a former all-America who is now in the NFL Hall of Fame:

"I'm just delighted for him. I'm so pleased that he chose to leave under these circumstances. He's still young and he's still healthy. He's decided to leave while he's still at the top of his profession. A lot of people are going to say this is a dark day for Michigan football, but I can only be pleased for Bo.

"People who only see Bo as someone storming up and down the sidelines don't really get a look at what he's all about. I had a chance to be at a foot-

Bo erupts in typical Bo fashion after an official's call during a 31-27 loss to UCLA in 1982.

ball reunion at Crisler Arena recently (in April 1989) and I saw so many of his former players. They all respect and admire him. I think that says more about Bo Schembechler than anything else. You see all these grown men with a look of total admiration in their eyes. They would still do anything for the man. It's the essence of what he's tried to accomplish. Anyone who's ever known him is the better for it."

Of course, he capped his career with a controversial, heartbreaking, 17-10 loss to USC in the Rose Bowl. Of course, he went out with a sideline temper tantrum in which he nearly hung himself on his headset wires. Of course, he went out in a blaze, ripping the gutless officials and the gutless administrators who put them there.

How else could this man go out? Quietly?

The play that drew Schembechler's wrath was when Michigan and USC were tied, 10-10, in the fourth quarter. On fourth and 2, Schembechler calls for a fake punt. Chris Stapleton, a freshman, pulls the ball in and runs 24 yards for a first down at the USC 31.

Behind the play, a late flag had been thrown. Holding. The play was nullified and Schembechler went off. He later would say he looked at replays all night, from all angles and saw no holding on the play.

"Then I later find out that all the officials were saying how they weren't going to take anything

Bo, unusually relaxed and upbeat, announces his retirement as U-M football coach in December of 1989.

(in 1996) but if I had to do it over again, I might have stayed on for two more years.

"I think I let the doctors scare me a little bit. They had been after me to slow down for some time. And the baseball thing (with the Tigers) was a complete disaster and a lot more taxing than I thought it would be.

"And, remember, I had two dominant football teams coming back in 1990 and 1991. I had an offensive line with (future NFL players) Greg Skrepenak, Dean Dingman, Steve Everitt, Joe Cocozzo, Matt Elliott and Tom Dohring. With that line you could have won whatever you wanted to win. I mean, I would have had a pat hand.

"And, plus, the new building (Schembechler Hall) was just built and I would have liked to sit in that (head coach's) office."

The Michigan teams of 1990, 1991 and 1992 — all teams with players brought to Michigan while Schembechler was there — won three straight Big Ten titles, and won in the Gator Bowl (1990) and Rose Bowl (1992). Michigan, through the 1995 season, hasn't won a Big Ten title since.

Bo reflects on his football career at poolside after his final press conference as head coach at Michigan.

Still Loyal to Mo

In May 1995, Schembechler was preparing to

get lost, to go someplace completely out of range of the fuss and frenzy of civilization. He was going fishing in a remote isolated area off the coast of Mexico.

While loading up his fishing gear, he was stopped dead in his tracks by a news bulletin on the radio. Gary Moeller, his faithful assistant through all those years at Miami of Ohio and Michigan and now his successor, had been arrested by Southfield police. Something about public intoxication, abusive behavior and causing a major disturbance at a fancy restaurant.

"My first thought was, 'Something is wrong with this,'" Schembechler said. "I've known Gary for years and he's a two-beer guy. Just like me."

His second thought was, "I have to talk to him."

He eventually tracked him down in a hotel room in Orlando, Fla., where Moeller had gone to attend some coaches' meetings.

After several failed attempts to reach him, Schembechler left a voice-mail message: "Listen, I'm leaving for Mexico in the morning but I'll be at this number all day and night. Call me. I don't give a damn what time it is. Gary, don't do any-

Bob Hope (left), Rose Bowl Queen Yasmine Delavari and Bo huddle prior to the 1990 Rose Bowl.

thing until you talk to me."

Moeller never called.

"When I was down in Mexico a couple of days later, I picked up a two-day old copy of USA Today," Schembechler said. "(Michigan athletic director) Joe Roberson was quoted in there saying that the incident would not cost Moeller his job. So, I was relieved, you know, and I sort of forgot about it. Then I get back and I find out that he resigned."

Schembechler smelled a rat. No way would Moeller give up that job without a fight. Something must have happened. Somebody, maybe the president of the university, wanted to make an

example out of Moeller.

Schembechler talked to Roberson. He talked to President James Duderstadt. He talked to Rich Hewlett, one of his former players who was handling Moeller's legal claims. Nothing that he was told allayed his suspicions, but nothing he could say or do could change what had happened.

"Something happened there that I am not aware of and, really, it breaks my heart," Schembechler said. "Now, I didn't listen to the police tapes or anything like that, but I know Gary Moeller. And this incident is so foreign to anything I've ever known about him. He's no carouser. He's not a womanizer. He's not any of the things they were accusing him of. And as I sit in this chair today, nothing like that will ever happen to Gary Moeller again."

Just as he did for Woody Hayes, Schembechler will defend Moeller for the rest of his days. It's what you do for people you care about. It's called loyalty.

"Maybe, I don't know, maybe the pressure got to him. There is a hell of a lot of pressure in that job today, way more than when I coached."

Schembechler, his eyes red and moist, shakes his head.

"I just wish I could have talked to him before he resigned. I wish, hell, I would have told him to hang in there. I would have told him to fight."

True Blue

In June of 1996, Bo's 1971 team had a 25th reunion. Again, just about every player, walk-ons and all-Americas alike, attended.

"At the same time, the Michigan basketball program had a reunion for Johnny Orr," Schembechler said. "Every kid that played for Johnny Orr was invited to that dinner. They had nearly as many guys as we had, and Johnny Orr never showed up. All those guys were in a room next to us, and they were all commiserating, so we invited them to come over and join us.

"So all these basketball players come over and we get to talking. And they're saying, 'You know, when you talk to a football guy from here, man, they got a look in their eyes. You know it was something special. We don't have anything like that in basketball. Why can't we build something like that in basketball?'

"I looked at him and I said, 'Let me ask you

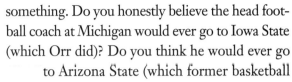

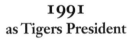

1991
as Tigers President

something. Do you honestly believe the head football coach at Michigan would ever go to Iowa State (which Orr did)? Do you think he would ever go to Arizona State (which former basketball coach Bill Frieder did)?' Hell no, he isn't going because he knows damn well he's got the best job in the United States. That's the difference. They don't have the same respect for the program."

Still In Charge

Bo Schembechler, with his jaw jutted, teeth clenched, fists balled and poised to slam the cluttered, unsuspecting desktop, leans forward, toward the desk in his office.

"Let me tell you something," he says, chomping on each word. "In college football today, it's no longer good enough to win a conference championship. It's no longer good enough to win a bowl game. At the end of the season, there is only one guy in the United States of America who's happy. One guy. Dammit, that's tragic."

This could have been one of those precious Monday afternoon press luncheons at Weber's Inn in Ann Arbor, where Schembechler once held court on any and all topics. It could have been one of his legendary postgame tirades. This could have been old General Bo, his Michigan football program at the height of its glory and he at the height of his power, admonishing the press, or his team, or the powers that govern college football.

This could have been 1976. Or 1986.

But it's not.

It's the summer of 1996. Schembechler is 67 years old and seven years have passed since he resigned as head football coach at the Michigan.

Bo and Detroit Tigers manager Sparky Anderson at spring practice in Lakeland, Fla., in 1990.

He is tanned and fit, and frankly looking younger than the dreary December day in 1989 when he announced his resignation from football. He is drinking a cup of coffee in his office on the second floor of Schembechler Hall.

"I have emeritus status," he says, somewhat sheepishly. "That's why I get an office."

Baloney. He built Schembechler Hall, raising $15 million in less than 12 months. He called it the Center of Champions (Schembechler Hall was the Michigan Board of Regents' idea and they pushed it through over Schembechler's protests).

"This was built for all the guys who played here in the past, the guys who built the great tradition of Michigan football," he said.

The building is a monument to Schembechler's legacy. It houses not only the football program, but its history. Within this building you can see where the program had been before Schembechler arrived in 1969, where it was when he left 21 years later, and where it has gone since he left. That he never sat in the head coach's office is a shame; to deny him an office altogether would have been criminal.

And from his messy, memorabilia-filled office, Schembechler, on the power of four annual golf tournaments, has by 1996 managed to raise $1.25 million for adrenal cancer research in the name of his wife, Millie, whose life was taken by the disease in 1992.

"Our goal is to endow a chair in Millie's name at University Hospital for one of the top adrenal

David Letterman listens to one of Bo's stories about Woody Hayes during a visit on NBC's "Late Night" in 1990.

cancer researchers in the country and offer a $2 million endowment," he said.

But on this day, Schembechler had his old game face on. His passion for college athletics has not atrophied in the seven years he's been away.

"With all due respect, the scariest thing about college sports today is that it's being run by people who do not know what it's all about," he said. "And these are the university presidents. They haven't the slightest idea what college sports are about or how they work.

"Every decision that is being made today is in the interest of money, not in the interest of the guys and girls who play. I resent that."

The trigger for this was the announcement that the Big Ten and Pac-10 conferences would give 50 years of tradition a swift kick in the rear by backing off of their exclusive hold on the Rose Bowl in order to help facilitate a true national championship game.

"I suspect this is a result of pressure put on the Big Ten by (Penn State coach Joe) Paterno and (Ohio State coach John) Cooper," Schembechler said. "These are two guys who simply do not understand the tradition of the Big Ten."

Schembechler shakes his head in dismay.

He's heard all the criticism about how college athletics have gotten out of control, how they need to be cut back. He's read where former U-M president James Duderstadt has called for the down-scaling of college sports to nearly pre-20th Century size.

Then he looks around Schembechler Hall. The athletic budget had grown from $21 million when he was athletic director in 1990 to nearly $40 million in 1996. He sees offices being manned by at least 10 "associate" athletic directors — most of them sent over from the university president's office without any background in college athletics. He sees where the athletic department has added a new female sport, crew, which will be funded by raising ticket prices for football games.

Then he reads where ABC has announced a multimillion-dollar deal to broadcast a national championship football game.

"I feel sorry for football coaches today," he said. "They increase ticket prices and demand the stadium be filled. They cut his grant-in-aides to 85 then complain about how he's exposing the freshmen players. They make him win a national championship and then they say there is an overemphasis on college football. Now, come on. Who is kidding who?"

These are not the emotional ramblings of a bitter, crabby old coach whose mind-set is stuck in some antiquated, Pollyanna vision of what college sports should be about. They are the emotions of a man who devoted his life to making college athletics the most enriching experience of a young person's life; a man whose heart is broken by the shattering of traditions and standards and values that he built his program and his life around.

As he stated in the forward to his 1989 book, *Bo: Life, Laughs and Lessons of a College Football Legend*: "The game has exploded. It's big money. It's big pressure and it's out of control. But it's still football, and as long as I'm here I'll coach it my way, thank you. I'll still scream at a freshman who fumbles the ball during practice. I'll still suspend a kid who misses classes. And I'll still defend what I think

is the most important element: Not championships, not TV contracts, but that every kid comes out of the program with a diploma and a feeling he was part of something special.

"And the knowledge that his coach — who may have yelled and kicked and busted his ass — is now a friend forever."

That, truly, is Bo Schembechler's legacy. More so than his 194 victories at Michigan and 234 overall in his 27 years as a head coach. More so than his 85-percent winning percentage in the Big Ten. More so than his 13 conference titles, 17 bowl appearances and 17 Top 10 national rankings. More so than the 39 all-Americas and 97 first-team All-Big Ten players he coached. More so than the $15 million facility that bears his name. His biggest achievement, he'll tell you, is that most of the 650 players he coached succeeded beyond college and remained his friend.

Testament to that occurred in 1989, seven months before he announced his retirement. A banquet took place in honor of his 20 years at Michigan, and players from all 20 teams were invited. Two-thirds of those players attended.

Again he leans forward, but this time his voice goes soft, as if he's confiding a great personal secret.

"Let me tell you something. The day this stops being a meaningful experience for the guys who play is the day we ought to throw the whole damn thing out."

A Special Breed

He was the last of the one-named coaches. Pop, Woody, Bear and Bo. He stood for honesty, loyalty, discipline, toughness and fairness. He tolerated no cheating, no shortcuts. Twenty-one years and not a hint of a scandal. No recruiting violations, no steroids, no academic fraud.

When, in 1979, he learned that some of his players were involved with drugs, he suspended them and immediately instituted mandatory drug testing for all his players. This was years before the

Bo and his wife, Cathy, in the press box at Beaver Stadium at the Michigan-Penn State game in 1995.

NCAA started requiring them.

When, in 1984, 12 of his players were caught using a stolen credit card to make long-distance phone calls, he sent each one a letter plainly stating that their scholarships were presently null and void until they paid back all the money they spent on the bogus card. All 12 made fast restitution.

When the boosters started making demands, he turned them away. When the agents started showing up on campus, he broomed them. When players skipped class, he suspended them. When they had personal problems, he counseled and consoled them. None of those things had anything to do with wins and losses. None of those things gained him as much publicity as his sideline tantrums and his postgame tirades. But all of those things spoke to the core of what made Bo Schembechler special. His priorities were his players, his program and the university — not television networks, national media, Nike or the NFL.

You wonder if college football will see the likes of his kind again.

"I was a football coach," he said. "That's all. I was one of the guys and I hung around a long time. I was a hard-nosed bastard but I was honest. And I had some success. This was my last coaching job and I walked away with the Michigan stamp on me.

"When you talk about Michigan football, you can talk about Yost and Oosterbaan and Crisler. And you can throw Schembechler in there.

"Schembechler would be right proud that you do."

Bo's coaching record

Year	Team	W	L	T
1963	Miami (Ohio)	5	3	2
1964	Miami (Ohio)	6	3	1
1965	Miami (Ohio)	7	3	0
1966	Miami (Ohio)	9	1	0
1967	Miami (Ohio)	6	4	0
1968	Miami (Ohio)	7	3	0
1969	Michigan	8	3	0
1970	Michigan	9	1	0
1971	Michigan	11	1	0
1972	Michigan	10	1	0
1973	Michigan	10	0	1
1974	Michigan	10	1	0
1975	Michigan	8	2	2
1976	Michigan	10	2	0
1977	Michigan	10	2	0
1978	Michigan	10	2	0
1979	Michigan	8	4	0
1980	Michigan	10	2	0
1981	Michigan	9	3	0
1982	Michigan	8	4	0
1983	Michigan	9	3	0
1984	Michigan	6	6	0
1985	Michigan	10	1	1
1986	Michigan	11	2	0
1987	Michigan	8	4	0
1988	Michigan	9	2	1
1989	Michigan	10	2	0
Total		**234**	**65**	**8**

Schembechler won a pair of Mid-American Conference and 13 Big Ten titles and his teams played in 17 bowl games in 27 seasons.

MY BOY, BO

By Joe Falls

He'd had his first heart attack at the 1970 Rose Bowl and now he was well again, coming back as strong as ever. It seemed like a good time to write a book about how he did it. Bo Schembechler hadn't been the Michigan football coach very long, but he had seen a lot and done a lot, and he clearly had things to say. It just took a little time to convince him to talk about himself, something he never liked to do. I tried every tact possible and finally got him to agree to do a book.

I won him over with the old dodge: "Maybe it'll help somebody through their own crisis." I didn't like doing this because it was one of the oldest ploys in the writing business, but he went for it, and I felt good because I felt he had some things to say that could be an inspiration to others.

So now we are sitting in his office and he's doing a good job of remembering things — his growing up days in Barberton, Ohio, working as a graduate assistant for Woody Hayes, going into service and seeing a football game in the Southeast every Saturday in the autumn, becoming a civilian again and returning to Ohio State and, finally, his hiring at Michigan.

Many people think Millie was his first wife. I did, too, until I found out he had been married briefly to Hayes' secretary in Columbus. I knew we would have to mention it in the book.

As the tape recorder was turning, I said: "OK, we've got to talk about your first marriage."

He almost came out of his seat.

"No way," he said. "That's not going in the book."

I turned the tape recorder off. "Bo, if we don't put this in the book, people will wonder what else we've left out. It doesn't have to be long. This is a matter of integrity."

He looked at me.

Integrity.

A big word with Bo Schembechler.

He sank back into his chair and said: "OK. OK. Let's get on with it."

I turned the recorder back on and said: "What was your first wife's name?"

He looked at me again. He didn't say anything. The silence felt heavy.

"Bo. Your first wife. What was her name?"

He started rising out of the chair. He was pointing his finger at me from across the desk.

He began spluttering. "She ... liked ... horses."

And that's all he could tell me. She liked horses.

Amazing? Yes. Unbelievable? Yes. Incredible? Yes. But that was this man — an amazing, unbelievable, incredible man. He could tell you the blocking scheme he used in the second half of last year's game against Illinois but he could not remember the name of his first wife? Talk about priorities. Nothing came before football in the mind of this man.

Halfway through the book, Bo stood up from

Bo instructs guard Frank Titas before sending him in with a play against Vanderbilt in 1969.

his desk one day and said: "That's it! I'm not talking anymore. It's over. Done! Finished!" And he walked out of his office and never spoke another word into my tape recorder. I had to shift gears. I spoke to his wife Millie, his kids, his coaches, his friends, even Woody Hayes. I asked them to fill in the blank spaces, which they all did, and very easily, too. They all had something to say about this man.

I recall a day in Pasadena. It was the day after another Rose Bowl game. Another loss to the Pac-10. Bo never did well out there. It was the one blot on his record at Michigan.

It was a warm and sunny afternoon, a perfect day to get outside and see some of the sights of Southern California. Bo had given his players the whole day off. He kept them under wraps pretty well, but now he felt they deserved a reward and gave them 24 hours to themselves. That might not seem like much but it was a generous gesture on his part.

The players scattered — some going to the beach, some to the movie studios, some even to Mexico to see what it was like in another country. I'd finished my follow-up story and my wife and I were ready to go for a drive when we wandered into the cigar stand in the lobby of the hotel.

Who should be in there but Bo. He was looking at the pocket books on the shelf, trying to pick out a good one for himself. In that moment, I felt a sense of sorrow for this man.

Here he had built a terrific operation at Michigan. He was beating everyone in the Big Ten, recapturing the old glories for the U-M people. He gave them a reason to feel proud of their school again. He was one of the most celebrated coaches in the land, a man who had put his own imprint on the game of football that few had ever been able to do in such a short time.

Now he was looking for something to read — a way to kill the only afternoon he had off in probably half a year.

I thought: There's got to be more to it than this.

But there wasn't. He had played, and he had lost. He did not feel like having a good time. He was probably hoping he had film of the game so he could start looking at it and making plans for next season.

An odd bird? Yes. That's easy to say. But a very dedicated bird, and one as smart as they come.

I was always asked about Bo, why he was such a success. At first, I didn't know what to say. I'd tell them he worked very hard, but a lot of coaches work very hard. I could not say he was innovative because he never developed a strong passing game — the kind needed to win in Pasadena. I always felt that was his shortcoming in the Rose Bowl. He played half the game while the West Coast teams played the full game.

Anyway, I had to come up with a good answer and I settled on something that I feel is absolutely true to this day. I know of no man in my life who could sense a problem quicker than this man and get it solved almost immediately.

The way I put it was: "Imagine this big round table, and right in the middle of the table is this massive problem. Bo knew how to reach into that table and get it all cleaned up before anyone even realized there was a problem."

He was a man of conviction, and action. He made up his mind — bam! — and that was it.

He could do this because he had all the right qualities in his life. He was open and honest. He spoke nothing but the truth. He never cheated. He was not motivated by anything but doing things as well as he could and doing them correctly. He could be a hard, stubborn guy and his detractors always played this up. But he was a man of supreme integrity, and he could go after problems without fear of the consequences. That's because he was so straight. If he made a mistake, so what? It was just a mistake — not something he tried to put over on anyone.

One of his quotes stands out in my mind: "Any

player you have to buy isn't worth having."

Simple, straight logic. Bo Schembechler logic. Very powerful.

He came to us as "Glen Schems" back there in December 1968 — a man none of us knew. That's how he registered at the Hilton Hotel in Ann Arbor. He could have signed in as Ghengis Kahn and it wouldn't have mattered. He was completely unknown to us, and it was Don Canham's genius that brought him to Michigan. Canham saw in him a man of determination, dedication and devotion — a man of great potential. He hired him to the surprise of everyone in the state of Michigan. He even paid him $21,000 a year.

Van Patrick, the old announcer, broke the story on TV. He was close to Canham and got this exclusive when Canham asked him what he knew about this Bo Schembechler, the coach at Miami of Ohio. When I heard Patrick talking about it on the 6 o'clock news, I couldn't follow the story. I did not know who he was talking about. Bo Schembechler? I couldn't pronounce it, much less spell it. It couldn't be right. Not at the school that gave us Fielding H. Yost, Fritz Crisler, Bennie Oosterbaan and Bump Elliott.

What makes all this so interesting is that Bo Schembechler became one of the most recogniz-

After a 23-6 win over Washington in the 1981 Rose Bowl, Bo addresses U-M fans in Ann Arbor.

able football coaches in the land — a man who could deal at the highest level. Not only did he take his place with the Ara Parseghians, John McKays, Joe Paternos and Bear Bryants, but he became known in the political world, where mayors, governors and presidents talked about him. The giants of industry considered it an honor to talk to him on the phone.

He ran the Michigan program like the CEO of U.S. Steel.

But his love — always his first love — was the game of football, especially the practice field. He enjoyed Saturdays because that's where it all happened, but his true joy were the Mondays, Tuesdays, Wednesdays and Thursdays on the practice field. That's when he could get close to his players and teach them his way to play the game. He never tired of the practices, and this is why Michigan compiled such an impressive record in his years on the job.

He demanded excellence — and got it.

I loved his three-foot ruler. He would walk around with the stick in his hand and — whap! — a player would get it on the back of his legs or on his rump if he didn't do his job properly. Nobody ever got hurt. It was more of an embarrassment to have the head coach pick you out for this particular punishment. Imagine, grown men allowing their teacher to whack them when they didn't do their lessons right. Try that in our schools today.

What was so funny is that Jon Falk, the equipment manager, would keep a bag of rulers hidden in the locker room. When one would break, Falk would slip the Field Marshall another one.

The Bo-Woody relationship was fantastic. It was even larger than the Michigan-Ohio State rivalry. Some of it was silly. Some of it was serious. Looking in from the outside at these two strong-minded men was very compelling.

Hayes always tried to be the teacher, keeping Bo as his student. That worked for a while, until Bo created his own success at Michigan. One story you won't read in many places is what happened when Schembechler got out of the Army and went back to Ohio State to work for Woody. Woody promised him a job when his service duty was over.

Bo was thinking of an assistant coach's job. But when he showed up at Hayes' office, Hayes drove him downtown to the employment bureau and told him: "They should have something for you in there."

It was a cruel and thoughtless thing to do, but Woody was Woody. Who could explain him?

In time, Hayes needed Schembechler's help — his skill as a coach — and brought him onto his staff. As Bo grew in stature, he began standing up to Hayes. When he didn't like something Hayes was doing, he told him so. Nobody had ever told Hayes anything, but surprisingly, Woody would take it from Bo. One day, though, they got into it so heavily that Schembechler threw a chair at Hayes.

They developed a grudging admiration for each other. Hayes insisted that Bo play racquet ball with him on Sunday mornings. Woody was older and slower, and a whole lot fatter. Bo could handle him, though he never tried to show him up.

If they were playing two out of three matches and Hayes lost, he would say: "All right, now it's three out of five."

Then four out of seven, five out of nine ... until Bo would say: "Don't you think we'd better go to work?"

When they became rivals on the field, the electricity flowed in Ann Arbor and Columbus. They made the game larger than life. You watched them through your field glasses as much as you watched the game itself. You never knew what they would do — when the next blowup was going to happen.

Notice, please, what happened at the start of every game. They would meet at midfield to exchange pleasantries. They spoke. They smiled. They shook hands. But neither man ever stepped across the 50-yard line into the other's territory.

When Hayes was fired by Ohio State after striking a Clemson player in the Gator Bowl game, Bo was crestfallen. If he did not truly understand Hayes, he had great respect for him — for what he had accomplished and what he had to go through to create the kind of program he did at Ohio State.

One coach feeling for another coach as only coaches could feel about each other.

On the Sunday after Hayes' dismissal, Bo called Woody and told him he had to talk to him. He set up a meeting at the home of Doyt Perry in Bowling Green — about halfway between Ann Arbor and Columbus. Ferry had been their coach in college, a grand old man they both respected.

Bo drove to Bowling Green in a blinding snow storm. Woody did the same from Columbus.

Schembechler wanted to get one thing straight: Woody would have to apologize. This was a terrible moment for the old guy but he hadn't said he was sorry. Bo knew that an apology wouldn't change things, but saying he was sorry was the proper thing to do. He talked this over with Hayes for much of the afternoon. Hayes finally agreed to issue an apology. Bo drove home, unsettled by the events but feeling better that his old boss was about to do the right thing.

Hayes never apologized, and Bo was deeply disappointed that Hayes had given him his word and never followed up on it.

A lot of people felt Schembechler was a tyrant. Maybe so. I never felt that way. I knew he was a strong-willed man but I always thought his bark was worse than his bite. He could even rant and rave in front of the people in his office and it didn't bother them. They knew it would be quickly forgotten. When Gary Moeller did the same thing, they were appalled, and even frightened. Bo was Bo; hey, they knew he didn't mean it.

Bo simply did what he believed in. He was not always considerate of others. But again, they knew it was nothing personal and he would not carry on about it.

I know a lot of people at Michigan State didn't like him. They were always looking for flaws, some way to discredit him. They couldn't beat him on the field and so they would attack his character. Bo blew up enough to give them reasons to come down on him.

Bo Schembechler became such a strong figure that it was impossible not to have deep feelings about him. If you liked him, you liked him a lot. If you didn't like him, well, you could hate him.

What happened to him in the Ernie Harwell situation with the Tigers clearly shows the depth to which people felt about him. He was the guy who was on Ernie's side — the one who prevented his firing and got him an extra year as the broadcaster, at more money than he had ever earned at his job.

But when Harwell cried about the way the Tigers were treating him, Schembechler got all the blame. The people in my business shot him through the head.

The truth is that it was Jim Long, the boss at radio station WJR, who wanted to fire Harwell. But nobody knew him — who he was or what he did. Bo was the boss of the Tigers and it was more fun to blame him. And this is where Bo made a major mistake.

He took the blame because he felt he was the head of the organization and should be ultimately responsible for what happened with the ball club. Very noble, but not very smart.

Bo at practice prior to the 1990 Rose Bowl, his last game as Michigan's coach.

Bo got it from all sides — especially from his friends in East Lansing. They felt they finally had a reason to hold him up to ridicule. When the correct story came out — that it was Long, not Bo, who came down on Harwell — it didn't matter.

Bo had saved Ernie's job but nobody could believe it or wanted to believe it. In all my years as a journalist, I never knew a story that got more attention or a story that was so misrepresented. I felt this was a complete injustice, but good old Bo said: "Aw, what the hell. Who cares."

Bo greets U-M fans at Ontario Airport upon the Wolverines' arrival for the 1990 Rose Bowl.

TEN TO REMEMBER

Compiled by Bob Rosiek

Yost's, Crisler's and Bo's greatest games.

Michigan Crushes Stanford in Rose Bowl

Michigan's offense en route to another TD in their 49-0 defeat of Stanford in the first Rose Bowl game.

Special to The Detroit Free Press

PASADENA, Jan. 1, 1902 — Stanford was convincingly defeated, 49-0, by Fielding Yost's Midwest titans in the inaugural Tournament of Roses football game.

Michigan has now completed its wonderful season by vanquishing eleven great football teams, while scoring 550 points and holding their opponents to none.

For the first 20 minutes of the contest, Michigan showed little advantage over Stanford. On their first two series, Michigan failed to move the ball into Cardinal territory. Later the Yostmen attempted a pair of field goals which weren't successful; the first from 45 yards wasn't long enough and the second from 25 yards was blocked.

Late in the first half, Stanford mounted the most magnificent defense ever seen on a far western football field. Michigan's powerful offense had dri-

The Michigan squad crowded into a horse-drawn wagon for the Tournament of Roses parade.

ven down to the Cardinal 3-yard line with little effort and appeared to have a touchdown score cinched up. But on the next four plays Stanford's defense began to dig in.

On first down, the Cardinal forward wall stopped Michigan just four inches from the goal line. The Yostmen charged into the Cardinal line on the next two plays but were hurled back on each occasion.

Then with the spectators all on their feet in expectation, Michigan rammed into the line once again but the Cardinal defense stiffened and denied the Maize and Blue offense any penetration. After the play, the umpire set the ball 6 inches from the goal line.

Suddenly, a roar and a thunderous applause went up for the California boys.

Three minutes later, Michigan was back battering at the Cardinal goal line once more but the Stanford defense stopped them at the 1-yard line.

The 70-minute match was 25 minutes old before Michigan could score a point. Stanford, however, had already missed two field goals by this point.

But Michigan was too powerful, too quick, too

Difficult winter conditions forced Yost's squad to practice in the snow while on campus in December 1901.

tricky and too immune from injury for Stanford to endure the awesome Michigan smashing attack.

Stanford's men played like demons, but they were sapped from the preparation of the last few days. Six of the original Cardinal squad limped to the sidelines and fresh troops replaced them, but Michigan stormed on and redoubled the fury of their attack on Stanford's line.

Steadily, the score grew from 0-0 at the end of 25 minutes to 17-0 at the end of the half, and 49-0 at the end of the contest. When the game was finally over, Michigan's squad walked off the field singing and no one was injured.

Up until this contest, Iowa had been the most difficult game for Michigan.

During the game, Michigan rushed for 527 yards on 90 attempts, scored 8 touchdowns, kicked 4 field goals, and made one, for a total of 49 points. Willie Heston led Michigan with 170 yards rush-

ing on 18 carries. Stanford picked up 57 yards on the ground on 24 carries, missed two field goals and failed to score.

Michigan punted 21 times, gaining 858 yards while Stanford punted 16 times for 508 yards.

As darkness began to fall late in the second period, Stanford captain Ralph Fisher approached the Michigan bench offering to concede. This cut the final period short eight minutes, or surely Michigan would have put more points on the scoreboard against the Cardinals.

The 49-0 score speaks for itself. It caps a season that will be long remembered in college football history. Yost's Michigan squad won 11 straight games while outscoring its opponents, 550-0.

Score by Periods

MICHIGAN	17	32	— 49
STANFORD	0	0	— 0

Brilliant Use of Forward Pass Gives U-M Victory Over Gophers

Michigan utilized the forward pass for the first time late in the second half to end a scoreless duel with Minnesota.

By E. A. BATCHELOR
Special to The Detroit Free Press

ANN ARBOR, Nov. 10, 1910 — Two perfectly executed forward passes, each swift and sure as a rapier's thrust; two plunges into the Minnesota line, and Michigan this afternoon had beaten the Gophers, won the undisputed championship of the West, established her claim to be considered the country's best and proved the superiority of skill and cunning over mere strength.

With less than five minutes to play in the final quarter of a desperate, punishing, but at the same time thrilling game, the Wolverines saw the opening for which they had been looking ever since the battle began. They were quick to seize it.

More than 55 minutes of the fiercest football ever seen on the new Ferry Field, football so grueling and intense that nearly every other play rendered some athlete a candidate for the trainers' attentions, had produced no score for either side, and had left the ball in Michigan's possession on her own 47-yard line. With the timekeeper's watch rapidly ticking off the few precious moments that remained before the close of hostilities, it was up to Michigan to adopt some plan of action that would produce quick results if she wished to escape the misfortune of a drawn battle.

The forward pass was decided upon as the maneuver most likely to result in a change in the tide and it proved to be exactly what was expected. First, the ball was shot to Stan Borleske, Michigan's left end, who caught it neatly and dashed to Minnesota's 30-yard line before they nailed him. Right here Michigan outguessed Minnesota's defensive completely. The Gophers never anticipated that the pass play would be repeated. But it was, and with such success that Borleske lacked only three yards of the goal line when the desperate Maroon and Gold players dashed him to the turf.

First down and but three yards to go! Nothing short of a miraculous stiffening of the defense or the misfortune of a fumble could stop the advancing Wolverines now, and neither of these contingencies arose. Stanley Wells was called upon to make a path to the land of plenty behind the final chalk mark. On the first attempt he would get only a yard; with the Gophers, fighting with the courage of desperation and the fury of wild men, hurling themselves upon him before he well got underway. Again, Well's signal was called and the line of blue locked with the line of red. For a moment the result of the plunge was in doubt to the eager thousands in the stands, but suspense was short-lived. When Referee Hackett separated the gladiators, Wells was found hugging the pigskin to his chest, safely over the goal line.

Then the crowd cut loose. There had been cheering all afternoon; some of it spontaneous, some inspired by the perspiring yellmasters. But what had gone before as a noise would have seemed a mere whisper beside the great Niagara of sound that broke from thousands of throats when Wells fought his way into the territory behind the Gophers' goal.

Venerable professors, giddy freshmen, staid and usually phlegmatic businessmen, small boys, pretty girls and even sweet-faced old ladies stood up and howled until their vocal cords refused to emit another sound.

Down on the field the Michigan team, substitutes, coaches, band and everyone else who managed to pass the barriers and gain admittance to the inclosure set aside for the elite, swarmed out on the battleground, mingling in one wild, joyous shouting, hugging, handshaking mob. The crisp November air was alive with blankets, hats, musical instruments and even money, some of the shouters being so excited that they threw away regular cash.

It took some time for the officials, who had to preserve their dignity, however much they wanted to shout, to clear the field. When the last maniac had been herded to his placed on the sidelines, and the substitutes had gathered up the assorted trombones and bass drums, Michigan was given a chance to try for the point-after kick.

Neil (Shorty) McMillan, the little quarterback who handled the reins over that great Michigan team, booted the ball to Bill Edmunds, who heeled it. Then McMillan poised the oval for Fred Conklin and, when the latter got the angle just to his liking, he booted the ball squarely between the uprights. That made the score Michigan 6, Minnesota 0, which is the way it will endure through all the ages of football history.

Several minutes of playing time still remained. There have been times when the complexion of a game has been changed even as late in the day as this, but such occasions occur mostly in books featuring the exploits of Frank Merriwell and other reliable heroes. Nothing of the sort was in the cards for Minnesota this time and the game for all intents and purposes had ended when Wells crawled over the goal line.

The Gophers didn't quit, though, badly as things looked for them after Michigan scored.

A crowd of more than 18,000 jammed Ferry Field to view Michigan's long-awaited season finale against undefeated arch-rival Minnesota.

They received Lawton's kickoff and were making fair progress working the ball down into Michigan's region of the field when the timekeeper blew his whistle. In these last few minutes the visitors really opened up some new football for the first time in the game and were getting away with it rather well.

Although all the scoring of the game occurred in the last part of the final quarter and came with a suddenness that was like a thunderbolt from a blue sky, there was action every minute of the whole four periods. Both teams had several chances to score points and there were thrills strewn liberally throughout the battle.

Minnesota started out like a winner, taking advantage of a Michigan fumble in the first period and getting the ball to the Wolverines' 8-yard line before the defense stiffened and compelled Johnny McGovern to try for a field goal. McGovern's famous toe wasn't working well on this occasion

and he missed by a wide margin. This gave Michigan a breathing spell and enabled her to take the ball temporarily out of danger.

Before the end of this first period, however, there was another – and bigger – scare in store for the Michigan adherents. With the ball in Michigan's 25-yard line, big James Walker broke through like an elephant charging through a canebrake and blocked one of Lawton's punts just as it left his toe. Leonard Frank, a Minnesota end, was on the alert and he picked up the ball and carried it across the goal line without being touched. Gloom sat heavy on the Michigan thousands, while across the field in the Gophers' cheering section men were going mad with joy.

However, one of the officials had been touched by the ball while in play, so Michigan was permitted to try the play over again, based on the rule which says "that when the ball strikes an official, it becomes dead on the spot." George Lawton then punted out of danger and Minnesota's last real chance to make trouble had fled.

Costly fumbling by Michigan's backfield kept the Yostmen on the defensive for almost the entire first period. Then the nervousness passed – and with it the penchant for putting the ball in the air – and the Wolverines came into their own. From the beginning of the second quarter on, the Wolverines out-performed the Gophers; the newer style of giving them the advantage.

Coach Henry Williams's team exhibited wonderful power at times and its famous shift play was productive on a lot of short gains.

Michigan played the most open game that she had shown all season, using the forward pass time and again.

Dr. Williams practically ignored their new brand of open football until after Michigan had scored. Then they tried it in desperation, realizing that they had everything to win and nothing to lose.

Michigan appeared to gain strength as the game progressed, playing much better football in the third and fourth periods than in the first and second. The final quarter was the one in which superiority was most in evidence but the last few moments of the third stanza led up to some of the thrillers of the close. Just before third period ended, a forward pass, and some good line bucking and a

dash by Vic Pattengill enabled the Yostmen to move the ball from midfield to Minnesota's nine-yard line.

It was maddening to the spectators to have action halted at this exciting juncture because the period had ended, but the rules make this sort of thing necessary and there was nothing for the nervous ones to do but sit and bite their nails for the three minutes during which the gladiators rested.

Play began in the last session with the ball in Michigan's possession, first down, on Minnesota's nine-yard stripe. Here the Gophers gave their grittiest defensive exhibition of the day, stopping two plays directed at the line. Lawton then fell back for the field goal attempts but his kick missed the goalposts by a foot.

This turn of affairs gave the ball to Minnesota on a touchback and enabled them to get out of immediate peril.

Michigan later got possession of the ball at midfield and started the attack that was to turn Ann Arbor into a city of the insane and to hang crepe on the doors up in Minneapolis.

Score by Periods

MICHIGAN	0	0	0	6	—	6
MINNESOTA	0	0	0	0	—	0

Michigan Downs Ohio St. as Buckeyes Open Stadium

Michigan's 19-0 victory spoiled the dedication of the Buckeyes' new football cathedral, Ohio Stadium.

BY HARRY BULLION
Special to The Detroit Free Press

COLUMBUS, Oct. 21, 1922 — There is a great splotch on the brand new 80,000-plus stadium that Ohio State University, amid much pomp and ceremony, dedicated this afternoon.

And tonight the old town is raining with the cheers of the maddening throngs from Michigan, whose football warriors today lowered the proud Scarlet and Gray of the Buckeye school before a crowd never before equaled at a game on a gridiron of the West. If ever a triumph was sweet to the Wolverines, this victory, 19-0, this afternoon was. For three years Yost and his loyal followers have been burning for the revenge they achieved on this, the red letter day in all the history of the Western Conference.

Ohio State was whipped to a standstill, damaged as no team coached by John Wilce ever had been before, and there is a deep thick pall hanging over every supporter of the Scarlet and Gray. In one blow, the Wolverines whipped out the fruits of Ohio State's triumphant years; pushed back again the chesty Buckeyes, and while about it, jumped again on a position that will command the esteem of the West.

Before the third period was concluded it was a foregone conclusion that the Ohioans were over their heads against the dashing attack and defensive of the Wolverines and many in the vast throng began to make their way to the exits.

Those who stayed were struck with awe by the Yostmen's precision in executing plays. For once, the spirit of Ohio State was killed and her supporters were almost speechless with the horror of the catastrophe.

Walter Camp was in the press box. He came to see the greatest football field in the country, and the caliber of pigskin toters in the wild and woolly West.

He saw Kipke, a blizzard in action, Goebel, Kirk, Roby, Cappon, Muirhead and Uteritz outwit, outplay and with the help rendered by their mates virtually crush the Ohio State battle front that its legion followers boasted would win over Michigan through superior intellect, better coaching and psychology they believed was created by the three past defeats of the Wolverines.

Michigan gave them thrust for thrust and never was worried in a single exchange. Ohio tried every phase of football she knew, but seemed dumfounded when the men of Yost solved every trick and actually led the Buckeyes to their doom.

Michigan scored two touchdowns and a pair of field goals this afternoon. Paul Goebel put the Wolverines in the lead in the first quarter with a field goal from the Ohio State's 11-yard mark. In the final period, Harry Kipke booted a dropkick from the 38-yard line. The touchdowns came in between, in the second and third quarters.

Both touchdowns were scored by Kipke, the

All-America Harry Kipke proved to be a one-man wrecking crew against the Buckeyes. Kipke scored 2 touchdowns and kicked one field goal in a spectacular performance.

first one on a double pass that sucked the whole Buckeye team over to the left while Kipke, taking the ball from Doug Roby, sped around right end for 25 yards and the first Michigan touchdown scored against Ohio State in four years.

Ohio State had not fully recovered from that blow when in the third quarter the little blond marvel of the Yostmen speared a pass out of the air and evading a broken field ran 35 yards and desecrated the Buckeye goal line again.

Like a unit, the Michigan line constantly attacked the enemy. Her ends nailed the Ohio State backs almost in their tracks and the tackles, particularly Stanley Muirhead, were as venerable as the Rock of Gibraltar. And realizing early that Ohio State could do nothing to stop Michigan's charging defensive linemen from quarterback Vince Workman – who it is said, can hit a dime with a forward pass at 50 yards – the Buckeyes began to blacken the air with heaves.

Only once was Ohio State dangerous, but the alertness of the Wolverines' backfield thwarted her designs. This happened in the third period, the roughest spot in the whole game for Michigan and one where the Yostmen were confronted by two serious ordeals.

Ohio State had the ball on the Michigan 10-yard line, with fourth down and 2 yards to gain.

Workman elected to try a pass that fell safely in Wilmer Isabel's hands, but Steger tackled him so hard that the ball, slipping from his hands, fell into

Frank Honaker's. Just Frank Cappon stood between the Buckeye end and the Michigan goal and it looked as though the Michigan fullback would not be able to get past the Buckeye blockers. But he dodged two burly linemen, swung around in front of Honaker and brought him to earth. Kipke immediately kicked out of danger. Later in the quarter Workman, favored by a slight wind, kicked the ball dead inside Michigan's 5-yard line. The Wolverines tried one play around end to get away from the uprights and Kipke booted the ball out of danger again.

The Michigan contingent was on hand early – nearly 18,000 strong. Special trains from Ann Arbor and Detroit were loaded to the vestibules and the roads were black with automobiles, each draped in the colors of the Wolverine school. One party made the "grade" from the university seat of the Wolverine state in an ancient car of standard make and tethered the machine to a hitching post just outside The Deshler Hotel by employing a halter. The car, from front light to rear bumper, was smeared with yellow and blue paint – and with the same lack of care that a novice applies calcimine in a bungalow kitchen.

Victory for Michigan will mean "hell" in this place tonight.

Score by Periods

MICHIGAN	3	7	6	3	— 19
OHIO STATE	0	0	0	0	— 0

Oosterbaan Races 60 Yards To TD and Michigan Victory

Bennie Oosterbaan, Michigan's first three-time all-American, stretches to receive a high pass against the Gophers' double coverage.

By Harry Bullion
Special to The Detroit Free Press

Minneapolis, Nov. 20, 1926 — Michigan remains supreme on the gridirons of the West.

The Maize and Blue won by the smallest margin in which a football game can be determined this afternoon before 60,000 people on a snow-covered field, 7-6. It was a case of Minnesota's bad luck and Michigan's good fortune.

One fumble, a careless piece of work of which a sturdy Gopher back was guilty, cost Minnesota a victory that ordinarily she would have achieved. Minnesota pulverized Michigan's line on a march of 70 yards to a touchdown in the second quarter and Michigan appeared helpless in its efforts to get through, around or over the Gopher's forward wall.

But Michigan won because one of her alert

Benny Friedman pauses in mid-air to intercept a Minnesota pass in Michigan's 7-6 victory.

young men seized a fumble on the Minnesota 40-yard line and ran 60 yards to a touchdown. Melvin Nydahl failed to kick the extra point after Minnesota's touchdown, but Benny Friedman "booted" the ball squarely over the crossbar for Michigan.

Outplayed in every department of the game by a powerful and in a measure, a resourceful eleven, Michigan won because she was lucky. Yet the Wolverines might have made the score even more decisive had Louis Gilbert kept his feet after intercepting a forward pass just before the timekeeper's first-half gun.

Minnesota had just started a forward pass before the pistol was heard, and leaping high for the ball, Gilbert caught it with a clear hole ahead of him. The fleet Michigan halfback then headed for the goal and had covered all but five yards of the distance when he stumbled and a Gopher fell on him.

It was a tough way for Minnesota to lose, but for the same reason Michigan's victory was all the sweeter to the Wolverines. Twice on successive Saturdays, Michigan won because from the Wolverine caste a kicker came forth who booted the extra point when it was needed.

But Friedman's accurate toe would not have aided the Wolverines had it not been for Oosterbaan who alertly picked up the loose ball and ran 60 yards to paydirt. Oosterbaan was all alone, when Nydahl fumbled the pigskin. The Michigan end wasted little time in picking up the loose ball and carried it over the goal line.

Quick to rally to Oosterbaan's aid, the Michigan linemen started taking out tacklers until only Robert Peplaw was left unattended. But the fleet Gopher halfback never was nearer than five yards to Oosterbaan as they raced over the chalk marks. Running with free arms, Peplaw picked up enough ground on the Wolverine to make a dive for him, only to miss when Oosterbaan side-stepped him and crossed the goal line straight up.

That Michigan was clearly outplayed is attested to by the fact that she made only two first downs against 19 by Minnesota. Yet the Wolverines were so fortunate that they almost made two touchdowns on two first downs. In rushing the ball from scrimmage, the Gophers made 328 yards and Michigan in its two first downs advanced the ball 48 yards.

It was the eighth straight time that Michigan beat Minnesota and the Gophers are beginning to wonder what they must do to end the oppression by the Wolverines.

In this game today, Minnesota beat Michigan in everything but points scored. Only a game eleven that is Michigan's could recover from the mauling it absorbed in the second period and come back to survive to win one of the greatest football games ever played in the West.

Men with hearts less courageous than those of the young men who were fighting in this crucial battle of the season to keep Michigan's record unsullied in the west, were resigned to what seemed to be disastrous fate, as the Gophers ran their plays from deceptive formations, scattering the Wolverines all over the turf.

Nothing could stop the Gophers in that never-to-be-forgotten march of 79 yards down the field, with Peplaw, Nydahl, Harry Almquist, Harold Barnhart and Herb Joesting taking turns in ripping huge holes in the staggering defense of the Wolverines. But it wasn't Minnesota's day to win, no matter what that smashing backfield was capable. The recovered fumble by Oosterbaan and his run of 60 yards proved it beyond question.

Mute witnesses to the changing tides of battle was The Brown Jug, the most famous of college football trophies, on the sidelines. It will go back to Ann Arbor tonight to stay another year at least.

To each of the elevens the jug was a mascot, the Gophers scoring while it rested on a table on their side of the field and the Wolverines matching the touchdown when the trophy rested on the other side.

From the shift formation, Joesting, Almquist, Barnhart and Peplaw bent and broke the Michigan line repeatedly in the first quarter, but when danger threatened, the blue-jerseyed young men stiffened and altering the Gophers' plan of attack forced a kick and took possession of the ball.

Throughout the first quarter Minnesota had the

Oosterbaan was voted to college football's All-Time team in 1951.

advantage as long as the Gophers adhered religiously to their running and plunging attack. Resorting to the passing game, Minnesota invariably lost the ball and a resounding kick by Gilbert sent the pigskin back deep into the maroon and gold's territory.

But the power of the Northmen could not be so easily thwarted. Shortly after the second quarter opened, Barnhart caught a punt on the Minnesota 30-yard line, where he was nailed in his tracks by two Michigan tacklers. This is the last time that Minnesota would be was stopped en route to the Wolverines' goal, which Joesting crossed on a short plunge after a steady march of 70 yards downfield. There was deception as well as drive in Minnesota's smashing line plays.

Frequently the hard running, vicious backs went catapulting past the secondary defense and Michigan only prevented their escape to the goal line by pulling the runners down from behind.

Not since Michigan used to be piled up on a gridiron in the lean days of Fielding Yost's regime has another eleven torn its line asunder as it was distributed over the chalk marks on that drive of 70 yards in the second quarter. Never did the Gophers fail to gain. On a drive into the sorely oppressed Maize and Blue line the bullet backs always made a yard or more. Once it was necessary for the head linesman to take the measurement to determine the first down, but it was over the required distance and the march continued.

John Molenda was bruised and battered from coming up to the scrimmage line in a brave but fruitless effort to stop the advance and Leo Hoffman relieved him as the Gophers slowly but steadily got nearer to the goal line. In all that time Michigan's only glimpse of the ball was when it appeared under the protecting arm of a charging Gopher.

Between halves the Wolverines got an opportunity to rest that they needed and the coaching staff devoted the necessary time to correcting the faults of the line, or the parts of the game plan that could be pieced together. Temporarily, Yost's halftime oratory had the desired effect, since in the early stages of the third quarter, it stopped the Gophers' line plunging and forced them to kick. Oosterbaan cut in and blocked the ball which Ray Baer recovered on the Minnesota 20-yard line. But

Benny Friedman, an all-America in 1925 and 1926, connected with Oosterbaan on many memorable passes.

the Minnesota forward wall that opened the holes in Michigan's line to let the backs through hurled back the Michigan attack and on fourth down Friedman's pass to Oosterbaan behind the line was incomplete.

Taking the ball out to the 20-yard line, Minnesota smashed through for two first downs and created the impression that another offensive parade was in order. But Michigan stiffened again, forcing Minnesota to kick. It was apparent that the Gophers were cherishing their 6-point advantage of six points and were prepared to protect it. This was evident from the fact the Gophers, if they had three yards to go on third down, chose to kick in spite of the fact that three yards on a plunge meant nothing to them in their sensational march of 70 yards in the second period.

Michigan never stopped trying nor slackened its hopes, however. Michigan knew that their "break" would come if they were patient. Frequently the pigskin was permitted to slip out of the grasp of a Gopher, only to have one of them recover. But the fatal fumble was to happen. Minnesota let the ball loose once too often and an alert Wolverine turned it into a touchdown.

Nydahl went crashing into the line, as he had done frequently before. But in the collision the ball was knocked out of his arms and was exposed to the agile hands of Oosterbaan.

Scooping up the leader on his 40-yard line, Oosterbaan turned and sprinted 60 yards across the sacred Minnesota goal line.

Score by Periods

MICHIGAN	0	0	0	7 —	7
MINNESOTA	0	6	0	0 —	6

Harmon Tops Grange's Record in Win Over Ohio St.

Tom Harmon cuts back against the grain against the Buckeyes. His Heisman performance (3 rushing and 2 passing touchdowns) led the Wolverines' 40-0 rout of Ohio State.

BY JOHN N. SABO
Special to The Detroit Free Press

COLUMBUS, Nov. 23, 1940 — In a glorious climax to the greatest football career of modern times, Tom Harmon and his Wolverines annihilated the Ohio State Buckeyes, 40-0, this wet November day as 73,648 rain-soaked spectators looked on in absolute amazement.

When Harmon & Co. had finished this football funeral in Ohio Stadium, Ohio State had suffered its worst defeat in 35 years. Not since 1905, when Michigan beat the Buckeyes by an identical 40-0 score had an Ohio State team been beaten so completely and unquestionably.

Harmon finished his collegiate career by surpassing every Big Ten football player of modern times, including Red Grange. Harmon scored 22 points over a slippery turf. He made three touchdowns, passed for two others and kicked four extra points.

Today's 22 points brought Harmon's three-year total to 237. His three touchdowns made his total 33, compared to the 31 which Grange scored while galloping for the Illini.

Harmon, a one-man club today if one ever existed, finished his career on the same turf that Grange did in 1925. But he was greater than Grange. In his final college game in 1925 Grange did not score a touchdown but gained 277 yards rushing and passing. Harmon made that record look pale.

The Michigan all-America netted 149 yards rushing. He completed 11 passes for 148 yards.

That's a total of 297 yards. He had a hand in five touchdowns. But that's not all.

Harmon did all the Michigan punting with a wet ball and averaged 50 yards.

He did all of the passing, plenty of blocking and furnished some smart tackling. He simply dissected the Ohio State team which only a year ago had been the Scarlet Scourge that swept to the Big Ten championship.

When Harmon left the field after his third touchdown dash of the day, with only 38 seconds remaining to be played, the whole crowd, friend and foe alike, stood up and cheered.

As Harmon left, the Michigan section of the stands emptied. Ten thousand Michigan rooters mobbed Harmon and formed a guard of honor to escort him to the locker room.

As evidence of the one-sidedness of this game, consider these facts: Harmon's three touchdowns came on runs of seven, 18 and seven yards. He

Harmon attempts a field goal against the Buckeyes.

With this interception, the Michigan defense shuts down the Buckeyes once more. It would be a familiar sight all afternoon.

passed 17 yards to Forest Evashevski for one touchdown and 16 yards to end Ed Frutig for another. He also kicked four extra points.

Harmon also did some fine blocking in the first period when another senior, Paul Kromer, exploded with the longest touchdown run of the day. Kromer took a punt by Don Scott and went 81 yards for the second Michigan touchdown. That was the only touchdown on which Harmon didn't handle the ball, but he knocked down two Ohio State players with fine blocks on this dash.

Ohio State, beaten in three other games, had dreams of redeeming itself when this game started in a cold drizzle. The largest Buckeye crowd in five years was on hand in hopes of seeing Ohio State salvage some glory from this sorry season. When

the battle was over, the Buckeye fans had forgotten about their football team and were cheering Harmon.

Francis Schmidt, the Buckeye coach, sat on that cold, wet Ohio State bench. He sat, winced and wondered wondered where he would be coaching next year. Harmon & Co. not only took all the punch out of the Buckeyes but punctured an Ohio State line which averaged 213 pounds so full of holes that it looked like a touch-football line.

Statistically Michigan's supremacy over the dazed Buckeyes was just as one-sided as the final score indicates. Michigan made 22 first downs to 6 for Ohio State, 299 yards rushing to 82 and 148 yards passing to 33.

All Ohio State had to show for 50 minutes was

the biggest Buckeye headache in 35 years.

Not once was the woefully weak Ohio State team inside the 20-yard line.

Whatever trepidation was in the minds of Michigan supporters at kickoff time was extinguished pronto. Michigan scored in every period, led 20-0 at the half, and simply toyed with the Buckeyes at the finish.

Harmon & Co. started puncturing the Ohio State line quickly. In the first quarter Harmon and his mates bent, ripped and then crushed the 212-pound Buckeye line on an 80-yard touchdown drive.

This drive took 11 plays and Harmon finished it with a seven-yard dash through left guard.

At least five Ohio State players in white jerseys had their hands on Harmon as he went for the touchdown 11 minutes after the start of the game. Harmon missed his the point-after try.

Exactly 69 seconds later Michigan resumed its scoring. This time Kromer took a high punt by Scott on Michigan's 19-yard line. Scott punted to Kromer all afternoon, not wanting Harmon to get his hands on the ball any more than necessary.

But Kromer was just as big poison on this occasion. He took the punt near the sidelines, cut completely across the field and headed for the goal line. Behind beautiful blocking, he went 81 yards. On the 6-yard line, Jim Langhurst, the Ohio State captain, made a do-or-die tackle and got only a mouthful of mud for his efforts. Kromer scored sanding up and Harmon kicked the extra point.

Just to show the bewildered Buckeyes that Michigan had more than a running attack, Harmon started passing in the second period. He rifled one pass to Evashevski which netted 17 yards and the third Michigan touchdown. This ended a 77-yard advance and Harmon booted the extra point.

Leading, 20-0, at the half, the Michigan boys continued their festival. In the third period Michigan took the kickoff and advanced 77 yards to another touchdown. This time Ed Frutig, playing his last college game, snagged a 16-yard touch-

down pass from Harmon for the finishing touch. Harmon's place kick was wide.

By this time nobody was thinking about the eventual outcome. Everybody was thinking about Harmon. So Harmon gave the boys and girls what they wanted. He scored two more touchdowns. He got one on an 18-yard end run which finished a 52-yard march in the third period. He added the next one on a seven-yard dash with only 38 seconds to play.

It was the last time Harmon carried the ball in his collegiate career and he carried it as Michigan expected him to – right over three men to a touchdown. Harmon added the extra point and then Davey Nelson replaced him.

This was Harmon's show, but there was a fine supporting cast. Fullback Bob Westfall did his share. He gained 130 yards net rushing, 48 more than the entire Ohio State team gained. He slammed through that line with a consistency which certainly shocked the Buckeyes.

When Harmon was kicking up the mud, Westfall was bouncing through the line. It was like a one-two punch. Westfall softened 'em up and Harmon finished 'em.

The defeated Buckeyes have a lot of sad memories. It was their fourth setback of the year, the most defeats they have suffered since Schmidt became coach in 1934. When Harmon scored the first touchdown, that added to another miserable mark. It was the first time since 1890 that every Ohio State opponent had scored in one season. Seven previous 1940 foes had scored on the Buckeyes.

Michigan finished the year with seven victories in eight games and thereby clinched second place in the Western Conference. Only the 7-6 defeat at the hands of Minnesota kept the Wolverines from the title.

Score by Periods

MICHIGAN	13	7	13	7	— 40
OHIO STATE	0	0	0	0	— 0

Michigan Routs U.S.C. in Rose Bowl

The 1947 Dream Backfield: (left to right) Bump Elliott, Jack Weisenberger, Howard Yerger and Bob Chappuis.

BY BALDWIN HILL
Special to The New York Times

PASADENA, Calif., Jan. 1, 1948 — The University of Michigan's dazzling football machine capped an all-victorious season today by slashing almost at will up and down the Rose Bowl greensward to defeat the University of Southern California, 49-0.

93,000 spectators, headed by General Omar Bradley, the grand marshal of the Tournament of Roses, saw Fritz Crisler's gridiron supermen run up a score unparalleled since Fielding Yost's point-a-minute Michigan team massacred Stanford by the same margin in the first Rose Bowl game in 1902.

With this triumph setting a modern Rose Bowl scoring record the Wolverines challenged Notre Dame's claim to mythical national gridiron supremacy.

With its twin offensive and defensive machines working so much like well-oiled parts that their intermittent replacements of each other on the field even were almost imperceptible, Michigan struck for a touchdown before the first period was ten minutes old.

During a Hollywood visit prior to the 1948 Rose Bowl, actress Marlene Dietrich poses with Wolverine stars Bump Elliott (left) and Bob Chappuis (right).

While Southern California struggled vainly to get possession of the ball for a decisive hitch, Crisler's wolfmen crossed the Trojan goal line – once in the first period and twice in the second period. They coasted along on a single tally in the third, but closed with a crescendo of three scores in the fourth period.

Each touchdown was neatly converted by the adroit toe of Jim Brieske, with Gene Derricotte holding. Their last two successful efforts set a new Rose Bowl extra point record.

Other records also were shattered. It was U.S.C.'s worst defeat in sixty gridiron years.

Michigan's total yardage – 491 – topped the mark of nearly twenty years standing set by the Trojans against Pittsburgh in 1930 – 427.

This was the twenty-fifth actual bowl game and the thirty-fourth staged in connection with the annual Tournament of Roses. The weather was bright and balmy, with just enough briskness.

The Trojans fought valiantly, with nary a hint of despair or dispirit, but were manifestly outclassed. The Wolverines' passes, chiefly from the talented fingers of Bob Chappuis, darted like precise bolts of lightning, and their plunges along the ground were like piledrivers. Trojan coach Jeff Cravath's previously spectacular outfit, by contrast, seemed to move in slow motion.

U.S.C. never could generate the power to get a consistent touchdown drive started.

Efforts to fight her way out aerially were unavailing, too.

Three Wolverine jackpots were rung up by fullback Jack Weisenburger and two resulted from passes by all-America halfback Chappuis to halfback Chalmers (Bump) Elliott and quarterback Howard Yerges, respectively. One touchdown was on a pass from halfback Hank Fonde to Gene Der-

Fritz Crisler and his Wolverine team at practice prior to the 1948 Rose Bowl.

The Michigan team gathers to board the train for their journey to Pasadena.

ricotte, who replaced Chappuis in the final quarter, and the finale on a pass from Yerges to Dick Rifenburg.

Tactics starred rather than strategy. Crisler used his regular single-wing variations throughout the game, while Cravath's men stuck to the old and previously reliable T.

Michigan won the toss, received, and yielded possession of the ball momentarily before embarking on a 63-yard, eleven-play drive. Sparked by Chappuis' flings, the Wolverines made the first score on a 1-yard plunge by Weisenburger.

As the first quarter neared its close, Weisenburger punted from his 47 out of bounds on Troy's half-yard line. That put U.S.C. in a corner where it had to kick out for safety and set up another Wolverine touchdown drive.

Going into the second stanza, Chappuis sent a 15-yard heave to Bob Mann, the fleet left end, for a first down on Troy's 26. One play later Chappuis

spiraled one 22 yards to Yerges on the four, from where he battled his way to the 1. Weisenburger barreled over left guard for the Western Conference champions' second tally.

Goaded into redoubled efforts, the Trojans drove from their 12 clear to Michigan's 10 on more than two dozen bitterly–fought plays, only to lose the ball when quarterback George Murphy's pass was intercepted by Michigan's Dick Kempthorn.

Then the Wolverines went eighty-three yards in eight plays. Elliott made the third touchdown on an eleven-yard Chappuis pass.

Early in the third quarter Weisenburger and Chappuis spearheaded another apparent touchdown drive that was thwarted by a fumble by Yerges on the 9, which was recovered by Walker McCormick, the Trojan center. However, U.S.C. again floundered, and Dean Dill punted at midfield to Derricotte, who returned 12 yards.

Failing to gain a first down, Weisenburger

Bump Elliott (left) and his brother, Pete, were both standouts for Fritz Crisler's powerhouse Wolverines.

punted into the end zone, and Troy started its third scoring try of the third quarter. On the second play, fading back to pass, Dill was smothered by the Michigan forward wall and fumbled.

Don Dworsky, the Michigan center, recovered on the 18. One play later Chappuis tossed to Yerges on the 13, and he went all the way.

In the final quarter Michigan, in possession of the ball thrice, capitalized each time. Going fifty-four yards in five plays, the Weisenburger-Chappuis combination scored with the fullback bucking the final yard. A Trojan fumble on the U.S.C.

45 was recovered by Joe Sobeleski, the Michigan guard, and diminutive Hank Fonde passed to Derricotte, who raced 21 yards for No. 6.

The final score resulted from two passes. Derricotte threw to Ford on the 40, and he drove to the 28. Then Yerges rifled one to Rifenburg, who made a sensational snare on the 7 and tallied.

Score by Periods

MICHIGAN	7	14	7	21	— 49
U.S.C.	0	0	0	0	— 0

Inspired Michigan Upsets #1 Buckeyes

Michigan captain Jim Mandich (88) and Ohio State's captains enter the field just moments before the kickoff of the greatest game in Michigan's storied football history.

BY CURT SYLVESTER
Special to The Detroit Free Press

ANN ARBOR, Nov. 22, 1969 — Call it a miracle or just call Michigan the new super team of the Big Ten.

Either is just fine, thank you.

The Wolverines defeated the best college football team in the country, the Ohio State Buckeyes, 24-12, Saturday in one of the proudest moments in Michigan's long and bitter rivalry with Ohio State.

The victory, in front of a record 103,588 in Michigan Stadium and millions on television, gave Michigan the Rose Bowl trip, a tie for the Big Ten title with the Buckeyes and avenged last season's disastrous 50-14 loss at Ohio State.

The Big Ten athletic directors made it official

a few hours after Saturday's result by naming the Wolverines to represent the conference in Pasadena on Jan. 1.

The Wolverines will meet Southern Cal in the grand-daddy of bowls. U.S.C. rallied to beat U.C.L.A., 14-12, Saturday and qualified for an unprecedented fourth straight visit to the Rose Bowl.

The Buckeyes came to Michigan with a 22-game winning streak, 17 straight Big Ten wins and the title of "best college team ever."

But the Wolverines, led by tough little Barry Pierson and unshakable Don Moorhead, simply beat it out of them – the winning streaks, the No. 1 ranking and the undisputed Big Ten title.

Pierson made three interceptions at defensive halfback and returned an Ohio State punt 60 yards to set up the touchdown that broke the game open for Michigan in the first half.

Moorhead completed 10 of 20 passes, gained 67 yards rushing and looked more like Rex Kern than Rex Kern as he directed the inspired Wolverines to victory.

Michigan fell behind twice in the first half as the Bucks scored on a one-yard run by fullback Jim Otis and a 22-yard pass from Kern to Jan White.

But the Wolverines came back with a pair of touchdowns by their own hard-hitting fullback Garvie Craw on runs of three and one yards, a two-yard burst by Moorhead and a 25-yard field goal by Tim Killian.

There were other contributors: sophomore tailback Billy Taylor with 84 yards, including a beautiful 28-yard run that helped Michigan come from behind for the last time; Craw, who gained 56 of the hardest yards in the game, through the mid-

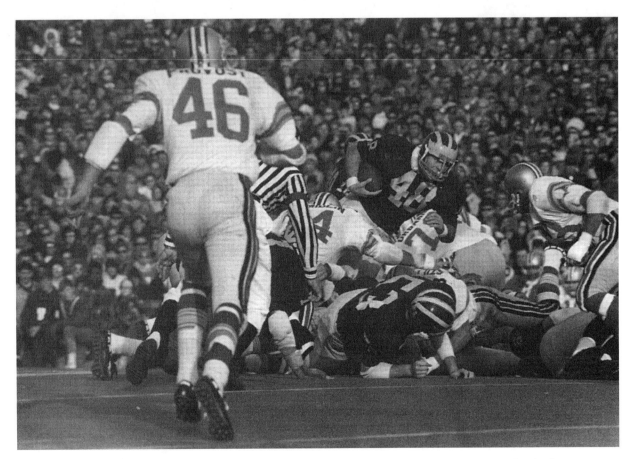

Garvie Craw (48) bursts up the middle for the Wolverines' opening touchdown against the Buckeyes.

Jim Mandich (88) turns upfield against the Buckeyes after a pass reception.

dle of the Ohio State line; flanker John Gabler and tailback Glenn Doughty who showed the Bucks some speed in the fourth quarter.

What the Wolverines did was to beat the Buckeyes at Woody Hayes' own game. They simply overpowered him and they simply out-defensed him.

That, probably, is not too surprising. Michigan coach Bo Schembechler learned a lot of his football under Hayes a few years ago and he obviously learned it very well.

Schembechler took Michigan into the game knowing it could not make a mistake and hope to win. The Wolverines made mistakes, but not until they had a two-touchdown lead in the first half and they forced Ohio State to make more.

Instead of Ohio State forcing mistakes as they had all season against weaker opposition, Michigan was forcing mistakes on Ohio State.

The Wolverines intercepted six Ohio State passes while Moorhead had only one pass intercepted. Ohio State fumbled twice and lost one. Michigan didn't fumble.

"We knew we were going to win from the very beginning," said Schembechler. "We said after Iowa we were going to win."

And that they did. The only disappointment for the Michigan fans was that the Wolverines didn't score a touchdown in the final minutes of the game

Dan Dierdorf cleared many of the holes for Garvie Craw, Don Moorhead and the other Michigan backs to rip for big yardage against the Buckeyes.

so they could have gone for two points as Hayes did in last year's game.

But the 24 points of the first half were all the Michigan defenders needed. The guys up front – middle guard Henry Hill, tackle Pete Newell and linebacker Marty Huff – kept Otis under control, although the O.S.U. bulldozer finished the game with 144 yards.

The defensive ends – Cecil Pryer and Kill Keller – kept the pressure on Kern and then his replacement, Ron Maciejowski. And the defensive backs had a field day.

"Pierson's performance was one of the greatest I have ever seen," Schembechler raved.

The little 175-pounder made three interceptions, four unassisted tackles, helped out on another tackle and treated the charging Otis with scorn, knocking his feet out from under him in the open field once and then pulling him down by the head on another occasion.

Tom Curtis, the Wolverine's senior safety, intercepted two passes and broke the N.C.A.A. record on interception return yardage, bringing his three-year total to 431 yards on 25 interceptions and erased the old national mark of 410 held by Michigan State's Lynn Chadnois.

Wolfman Tom Darden also made an interception and linebacker Mike Taylor broke up a pass.

When the game started it looked like Ohio State

might be on its way to another easy victory much like the first eight of this season.

Kern ran for 25-yards on the first play of the game and Otis went seven on the second.

But the Wolverines stopped the drive on their own 10-yard line.

The Bucks did score on their next series after Larry Zelina returned a Michigan punt 36 yards to the Wolverines' 16. Kern hit White for a 13-yard gain and Otis crashed over on his third bolt into the line.

O.S.U.'s Stan White missed the extra point and the Wolverines began to work.

Doughty took the kickoff and returned it 30 yards to the Wolverines' 45. Moorhead put the drive in motion with an eight-yard pass to split end Mike Oldham and a seven-yarder to Jim Mandich.

The Michigan quarterback hit Mandich again for nine yards and then Gabler ran for 11 yards on a counter play. Moorhead ran for six and then Craw went over from the one.

Frank Titas' extra point kick put Michigan on top, 7-6, with 3:35 left in the first quarter.

The Bucks began moving again, but now it was primarily on the passing of Kern instead of the running of Otis. Michigan was called for pass interference once, then Kern hit White for 28 yards and again on a 22-yard TD pass.

Little did Hayes, as usual attired in his short shirtsleeves, realize that would be the last touchdown his team would score.

Doughty again got the Wolverines going, this time with a 31-yard kickoff return.

Moorhead followed with a pass to Billy Harris for nine yards, Gabler ran for seven and Moorhead hit Mandich for nine, giving Michigan the ball on O.S.U.'s 33.

Taylor then made one of his patented broken field runs, shaking off linebacker Phil Strickland, halfback Ted Provost, and safetyman Mike Sensibaugh as he rattled 28 yards to the Bucks' five-yard line.

Craw got four yards on his first try and one on his second, putting him over the goal line with 11:54 left in the half. Titas' kick gave Michigan the lead, 14-12.

The Bucks couldn't move the ball on their next try, and when they punted, Pierson made the catch and bucked the Buckeyes for 60 yards with stiff arms and footwork as he gave Michigan the ball on Ohio State's three-yard line.

Craw went for one yard and then Moorhead dived around right end for a touchdown, Titas kicked the point-after and suddenly Michigan was in command, 21-12.

The Wolverines scored again before the half ended as Killian hit a 25-yard field goal.

Curtis made two interceptions in the final minutes of the half as Kern tried desperately to get another TD.

Michigan also had one touchdown taken away. Moorhead hit Mandich in the end zone, but the Wolverines were charged with illegal procedure and Killian had to kick his field goal.

Michigan might have scored several touchdowns in the last half but the Buckeyes were still tough and they gave away nothing.

The key to the victory was the ability of Michigan to contain the O.S.U. offense during the last half of play. Otis continued to gain yards, but more often than not Newell, Huff and Hill were ready for him at the center of the line.

Kern was under tremendous pressure and yielded to Maciejowski in the final quarter.

Behind Maciejowski the Bucks finally crossed midfield but Pierson intercepted a pass and that ended the drive.

The victory left Michigan, the 17-point underdog, and Ohio State, the invincible, with identical 6-1 Big Ten records atop the conference standings.

Score by Periods

MICHIGAN	7	17	0	0	— 24
OHIO STATE	6	6	0	0	— 12

Stubborn Wolverines Storm Buckeyes, 22-0

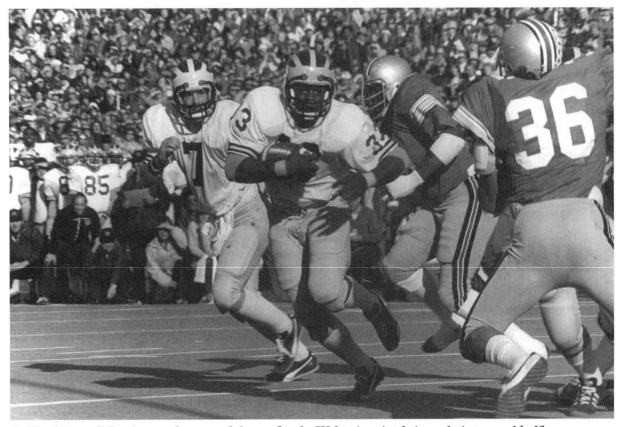

Fullback Russell Davis posted two touchdowns for the Wolverines in their explosive second half.

By Curt Sylvester
Special to The Detroit Free Press

Columbus, Nov. 20, 1976 — Goodbye, Ohio State jinx, hello Rose Bowl.

After four years of agonizing and mind-bending failures, the University of Michigan finally got the job done on Ohio State Saturday.

Not with flying footballs and heart-stopping field goals as the seconds slipped off the scoreboard clock.

The Wolverines did it their way – with an unstoppable running game and an unfailing defense – as they shoved Ohio State aside, 22-0, to grab a share of the Big Ten title and earn their first Rose Bowl trip since the 1971 season.

Ohio State gained a measure of consolation by accepting a bid to the Orange Bowl – the same bowl that Michigan went to as runner-up a year ago – against the Big Eight representative, yet to be determined.

Led by the rushing of senior Rob Lytle, the

All-America halfback Rob Lytle rambles for big yardage against the Buckeyes.

Lytle added Michigan's third touchdown in the fourth quarter. He finished the day with 165 yards on 29 carries.

Wolverines broke up a scoreless halftime tie with three second-half touchdown drives that never left the outcome in doubt.

No need for a tie-breaking touchdown, no need for a vote of the Big Ten athletic directors, no need to second-guess the play on fourth and one at the Ohio State goal line.

Those were the things that had spoiled it for Michigan for the last four years but they couldn't spoil it this time.

"We have always played well against them (O.S.U.), but the missed field goals or something have always held us back," exclaimed U-M coach Bo Schembechler. "But I felt going into this game we weren't going to be stopped."

And once the Wolverines got the Buckeyes loosened up in the second half – springing Lytle on option pitches, cutting quarterback Rick Leach inside and running fullback Russell Davis up the middle –

the Wolverines weren't about to be stopped.

Davis scored twice on three-yard runs in the third quarter and Lytle burst across from the same distance in the fourth.

Bobby Wood kicked two extra points and Jerry Zuver, the holder on extra points, ran a two-point conversion in the closest thing to razzle-dazzle you can expect to see from Michigan for along time.

All that was left to be done was the defensive mop-up and those hustling guys up front – Greg Morton, John Hennessey, Steve Graves, Tom Seabron and the rest – made it easy.

They pressured Ohio State quarterback Jim Pacenta relentlessly all afternoon and, except for a 24-yard run by Pacenta and a 21-yarder by tailback Jeff Logan, they were there to cut off the Buckeye running game.

The result was the first Ohio State shutout in 12 years, since Michigan turned the trick – 10-0 on the way to Pasadena in 1964.

It couldn't help but impress the 88,250 Ohio Stadium fans, who started wandering home after Michigan's final TD midway in the third period. Not to mention those millions who turned in on television that is, if they stayed awake through the first half.

As the coaches say, the first half was hard-nosed, defensive football; translated, that's a heck of a lot of bumps, bruises and punts.

Eleven times during the first half the punters had to exercise their skills. O.S.U.'s Tom Skladany booting six times for a 51-yard average and U-M's John Anderson kicking five for an average of 41 yards, as the teams traded field position and ran at each other's mid-sections.

"We didn't play a real good offensive game in the first half," explained Schembechler afterward, "We made mistakes, we didn't do what we wanted to do."

But the second half was another story.

Instead of going to the passing game as so many thought they'd have to, the Wolverines stuck to their ground game. But they livened it up with more of the option plays they had been using all season and it worked.

Michigan used up the first six minutes and 11 seconds of the second half on an 80-yard drive, with Leach running 20 yards on a broken play and cleverly drawing O.S.U. offsides with a long count to set up Davis' touchdown.

Not a pass was thrown in the drive, but U-M led, 7-0.

The TD succeeded in getting Woody Hayes mad but even that couldn't get the Bucks going.

Hayes felt that U-M tackle Billy Dufek Jr. had moved prematurely on the scoring play so he flailed the air momentarily. To no avail.

The TV replay indicated that Hayes might have been justified, but Dufek explained with a grin: "I was just getting off the ball quick."

Ohio State got off three plays and a punt, and once again Michigan was marching. This time the drive began at the U-M 48. A big 16-yard reverse by wingback Jim Smith and another 16-yard jaunt by Lytle, who finished the day with 165 yards, set up Davis' second TD run.

Again, not a pass was thrown and when Zuver finished his scamper into the end zone it was 15-0 for U-M with less than two minutes left in the third quarter.

"We felt 14 points weren't enough in this game," Schembechler said. "We couldn't go (to the Rose Bowl) with a tie, so we had to go for two. We put that play in just this week. The only question was whether we'd do it after the first or second touchdown."

The Wolverines were moving again early in the fourth quarter until Leach's only pass of the half was intercepted by O.S.U.'s Tom Roche on the Buckeye 13.

But Zuver came right back to intercept Pacenta's first toss and U-M was set up on the 16-yard line of O.S.U., ready to go for its convincing third TD.

The closest the Bucks came to scoring was late in the first half after Pacenta and Logan had escaped the U-M defenders, but Pacenta put the ball into the air in the end zone and defensive back Jim Pickens made the interception.

It was obvious from the celebration in the Wolverines' locker room how much it meant to beat the Buckeyes for the first time in five years, especially in Columbus with the stakes as high as they were.

"This has to rank with the great ones we've had," said Bo, "you'd have to go back to the 1969 game. We really won't feel the impact of this game until we get home with our friends."

But nobody could have doubted it. It was a celebration that many had waited years for.

And nobody was going to miss out.

Score by Periods

MICHIGAN	0	0	15	7	— 22
OHIO STATE	0	0	0	0	— 0

Anthony Carter (1) and Bo Schembechler are interviewed by NBC-TV's Merlin Olsen following a brilliant Wolverine win in the Rose Bowl.

Finally! Bo, U-M Win Roses, 23-6

BY MICK MCCABE
Special to The Detroit Free Press

PASADENA, Calif., Jan. 1, 1981 — As its fight song boasts, the Michigan football team is returning to Ann Arbor as true "Champions of the West" for the first time under Bo Schembechler.

And it was a passing attack that brought the usually running-minded Schembechler his first Rose Bowl victory.

U-M quarterback John Wangler and all-America wide receiver Anthony Carter hooked up just enough Thursday to complement the power running of tailback Butch Woolfolk and another strong defensive performance to lead U-M to a 23-6 victory over Washington.

It gave the fifth-ranked Wolverines (10-2) their first victory here since 1965 and the first after five frustrating losses under Schembechler.

"I've been here five times and five times I sat

here with my head between my legs," Schembechler said. "Now I can smoke a cigar and enjoy it."

It was the first time a Schembechler-coached U-M team finished the season with a victory and the ninth straight win for the Wolverines. And don't forget: this is the same U-M team that was 1-2 after three games this season.

"This football team has given us, the coaches, the fans – all of us – a great thrill the way they played," said Schembechler. "We played a great football team today. We felt going in they were a great team and they were. The thing that amazed me was that our defense still kept them out of the end zone." For the last 22 quarters, no team has managed to score a touchdown against a Michigan defense that returned only three starters from a year ago.

While the defense did its job, the passing from Wangler to Carter got the offense going.

In the first half, Carter did not catch a single pass and carried the ball once for two yards.

But the second half was a different story, as the sophomore wide receiver caught five passes for 68 yards and a TD. He also ran with the ball three times for 31 yards.

Butch Woolfolk (24) was named the Rose Bowl's M.V.P after a stellar performance of 182 yards on 26 carries and one touchdown.

The Wolverines' defense stops Washington at the goal line.

"John (Wangler) just hadn't gone to him," Schembechler said, explaining Carter's first half stats. "John felt if he did he would be forcing the ball. At halftime we told him to force it into him."

The Wolverines, who led, 7-6, at the half on Woolfolk's six-yard run, at first hardly resembled Big Ten champions.

"Every Rose Bowl we've played in we were down at the half," Schembechler said. "We felt if we were leading by a point and had not played well the game would eventually come our way.

"The other thing was that we let Anthony stand there alone long enough so we wanted to bring him into the ball game. When you do, things happen."

Carter was back when he caught a 27-yard Wangler pass to put the ball at the 11-yard line of Washington on U-M's first possession of the third quar-

ter. Four plays later Ali Haji-Sheikh booted a 25-yard field goal to make U-M's lead 10-6.

In the first half Washington quarterback Tom Flick completed 15 of 23 passes for 189 yards. But all that produced were two field goals by Chuck Nelson. In the second half the Wolverine defense limited Flick to eight of 16 attempts for 93 yards.

The Huskies came close to scoring in the first quarter when they ran four plays inside the eight-yard line. But they came up short when Toussaint Tyler was stopped inches from the goal line on fourth down.

Washington also got to U-M's 25 in the second quarter before Brian Carpenter picked off a Flick pass.

"We knew going in we would not get many opportunities, and when you got them you had to stick points on the board," said Washington coach

Don James. "Michigan has a great defense and we ran a lot of plays in the first half. They saw the plays and they reacted to them.

"They kept getting better."

On their possession after Haji-Sheikh's field goal, the Wolverines came back. Wangler passed 10 yards to Chuck Christian, 17 yards to Alan Mitchell and then 14 yards to Carter to set up the seven-yard TD pass to Carter.

Michigan sealed its win on Stan Edwards' one-yard touchdown run with 4:02 remaining. During the drive Carter carried the ball on an end around for 21 yards and caught an 18-yard Wangler pass.

Woolfolk, the only effective weapon U-M had in the first half, finished the game with 182 yards in 26 attempts. He also finished with the game's most valuable player award.

"This is the biggest game I've ever had," the junior tailback admitted. "We won the high school state championship in New Jersey and we won the Big Ten championship in my freshman year. But those can't compare to this."

Schembechler, who suffered a heart attack the morning before his first Rose Bowl game in 1970 (he later had open-heart surgery), was mobbed after the win, receiving a bloody nose from one of his own players during the celebration.

"By the time I got pounded on out there I could hardly breathe," he said with a smile.

"And I don't have the best of hearts."

He admitted he shed a few tears over his first bowl victory.

"I'm on top of the world in every respect," he said.

Score by Periods

MICHIGAN	0	7	10	6	— 23
WASHINGTON	0	6	0	0	— 6

Wolverines Pluck Irish Luck

All-America defensive back Garland Rivers (13) made life difficult for the Irish.

BY TOMMY GEORGE
Special to The Detroit Free Press

SOUTH BEND, Ind, Sept. 13, 1986 — Michigan took the gifts Notre Dame offered – three turnovers inside the U-M 15 – and muscled its way to a 24-23 win Saturday at Notre Dame Stadium.

And then with 1:33 left, amid a potential game-ending drive and after a turnover-free three quar-

ters, the Wolverines returned the favor. Bob Perryman fumbled at the Notre Dame 26 and linebacker Wes Pritchett recovered. Irish quarterback Steve Beuerlein then completed 33- and 16-yard passes to move Notre Dame to Michigan's 28. Seventeen seconds were left. Finally, in trotted Irish kicker John Carney.

"I turned to Mike Reinhold on the sidelines and said, 'Mike ... he's going to make it,' " said U-M

All-America quaterback Jim Harbaugh dueled with Notre Dame's Steve Beuerlein in an aerial battle that the Wolverines barely managed to win, 24-23.

quarterback Jim Harbaugh. "He said, 'Hey, suck in that stomach, Jimmy. No way. No way.' "

Carney's 45-yard kick had the distance but drifted left with 13 seconds left, and the thrilling finish kept the score intact – Michigan 24, Notre Dame 23 – before a capacity crowd of 59,075 and a national TV audience.

It was Notre Dame's 16th consecutive sellout and 113th of the last 114th games.

There were big plays and bigger controversies, but it wound up a season-opening victory for U-M, a crushing debut loss for Irish coach Lou Holtz.

"There are an awful lot of sad young men in our locker room right now," Holtz said. "We never seemed to have anything bounce our way the entire day. But hopefully this game will serve as a strong foundation."

Notre Dame's foundation would have been much surer had Carney's kick sailed more to the right, had he not earlier missed an extra point or had tight end Joel Williams been ruled inbounds on his apparent touchdown catch deep in the end zone with 4:26 left that would have given Notre Dame a 26-24 lead.

However, as Harbaugh said, "Good luck is the byproduct of hard work." And Irish turnovers on this day were their first steps to defeat.

Notre Dame made four of them:

• The first, two minutes into the second half when flanker Reggie Ward fumbled at U-M's 7. Safety Tony Gant recovered.

• The second, with 8:57 remaining in the third quarter, when the Irish did not pounce on a high, short Michigan kickoff and U-M safety Doug Mallory did, at Notre Dame's 27.

• The third, with a minute left in the third quarter, when fullback Pernell Taylor fumbled at Michigan's 15, recovered by Mallory.

• And the fourth, with 10:54 to play, when Beuerlein's eight-yard toss into the end zone was intercepted by cornerback David Arnold.

The crucial miscues were the interception and

the flubbed kickoff. Especially the kickoff, because Michigan had just erased Notre Dame's 14-10 half-time lead by taking the second-half kickoff, driving 78 yards and scoring on Jamie Morris' one-yard run. Mallory then recovered the kickoff. Harbaugh needed only six seconds to find Morris for a 27-yard touchdown and a 24-10 U-M lead.

The game's final points came on Williams' two-yard catch with 3:10 left in the third quarter (after which Carney missed the extra point) and Carney's 25-yard field goal with 4:26 remaining (after Williams was ruled out of bounds on his catch).

Notre Dame didn't punt once in nine possessions. It produced 455 yards, averaged 6.3 yards a play, had 27 first downs, and was eight-for-12 on third-down conversions. It was enough to make Michigan coach Bo Schembechler rub his eyes afterward in despair.

"I expect a better question than that," he said when asked about his defense. "But Lou Holtz is a very diverse offensive coach, and he kept us off balance with so many different formations. We were in hostile territory. We came out with a victory. I don't care how you come out with them."

Harbaugh, scrambling and passing on a variety of rollout plays, was 15-of-23 for 239 yards and a touchdown, and Morris rushed for a game-high 77 yards and caught three passes for 31 yards.

"I've never caught a ball that far downfield," Morris said of his touchdown grab. "It was a throw-back play, where the back just runs downfield down the sideline. That was a big thrill."

Notre Dame took advantage of a shanked punt and its swarming goal-line defense to lead at half-time, 14-10.

Michigan's offense controlled the ball for nearly 19 minutes of the half. Harbaugh was 7-of-9 passing for 101 yards, and his scrambling and roll-out passing helped Michigan to 203 yards, 11 first downs and three drives that covered at least 60 yards.

After Pat Moons missed a 42-yard field goal,

Wolverines assistant coach Gary Moeller and Bo on the sidelines

Notre Dame drove 75 yards, with Tim Brown scoring on a three-yard run. Michigan needed only 33 seconds to answer, however, as Morris shook three Irish tacklers on an eight-yard scoring run.

Two minutes into the second quarter, Irish flanker Reggie Ward fumbled and safety Tony Gant recovered at the Michigan 7. But Monte Robbins' shanked punt of 21 yards gave the ball right back to Notre Dame, at the Michigan 26.

Eight plays later, Mark Green dived one yard for a touchdown and a 14-7 Irish lead with 8:08 left.

Moon's 23-yard field goal made it 14-10 at the half.

Score by Periods

MICHIGAN	7	3	14	0	— 24
NOTRE DAME	7	7	6	3	— 23

APPENDIX

Compiled by Bob Rosiek

Michigan Football
Fielding Yost Era - All Time Team
1901-23, 25-26

Position	Name	Hometown	Year
End	Neil Snow	Detroit, Michigan	1901
	Stanfield Wells	Brewster, Ohio	1911
	Paul Goebel	Grand Rapids, Michigan	1922
	Bennie Oosterbaan	Muskegon, Michigan	1927
Tackle	John Curtis	Brooklyn, New York	1906
	Miller Pontius	Circleville, Ohio	1913
	Angus Goetz	DeTour, Michigan	1920
	Tom Edwards	Central Lake, Michigan	1925
Guard	Dan McGugin	Tingley, Iowa	1902
	Albert Benbrook	Chicago, Illinois	1910
	Ernie Allmendinger	Ann Arbor, Michigan	1913
	Butch Slaughter	Louisville, Kentucky	1924
Center	Germany Schultz	Fort Wayne, Indiana	1907
	Ernie Vick	Toledo, Ohio	1921
Quarterback	Boss Weeks	Allegan, Michigan	1902
	Benny Friedman	Cleveland, Ohio	1926
Halfback	Albert Herrnstein	Chillicothe, Ohio	1902
	Willie Heston	Grants Pass, Oregon	1904
	John Maulbetsch	Ypsilanti, Michigan	1916
	Harry Kipke	Lansing, Michigan	1923
Fullback	Tom Hammond	Ann Arbor, Michigan	1905
	John Garrels	Detroit, Michigan	1906
Placekicker	Tom Hammond	Ann Arbor, Michigan	1905
Punter	Harry Kipke	Lansing, Michigan	1923

Note: Player listings are chronological by position with final varsity season indicated.

Michigan Football
Fritz Crisler Era - All Time Team
1938 - 1947

Position	Name	Hometown	Year
End	Ed Frutig	River Rouge, Michigan	1940
	Elmer Madar	Detroit, Michigan	1946
	Bob Mann	Bern, North Carolina	1947
	Dick Rifenburg	Saginaw, Michigan	1948
Tackle	Merv Pregulman	East Lansing, Michigan	1942
	Alvin Wistert	Chicago, Illinois	1942
	Bill Pritula	Detroit, Michigan	1947
	Bruce Hilkene	Indianapolis, Indiana	1947
Guard	Ralph Heikkinen	Ramsey, Michigan	1938
	Julius Franks	Hamtramck, Michigan	1942
	Dom Tomasi	Flint, Michigan	1948
	Stu Wilkens	Canton, Ohio	1948
Center	Archie Kodros	Alton, Illinois	1939
	Dan Dworsky	Sioux Falls, South Dakota	1948
Quarterback	Forest Evashevski	Detroit, Michigan	1940
	Howard Yerges	Point Pleasant, W. Va.	1947
Halfback	Tom Harmon	Gary, Indiana	1940
	Bob Chappuis	Toledo, Ohio	1947
	Bump Elliott	Bloomington, Indiana	1947
	Gene Derricotte	Defiance, Ohio	1948
Fullback	Bob Westfall	Ann Arbor, Michigan	1941
	Bill Daley	St. Cloud, Minnesota	1943
Placekicker	Jim Brieske	Harbor Beach, Michigan	1947
Punter	Bob Wiese	Jamestown, N. Dakota	1946

Note: Player listings are chronological by position with final varsity season indicated.

Michigan Football
Bo Schembechler Era - All Time Team (Offense)
1969 - 1989

Position	Name	Hometown	Year
End	Jim Mandich	Solon, Ohio	1969
	Eric Kattus	Cincinnati, Ohio	1985
Tackle	Dan Dierdorf	Canton, Ohio	1970
	Paul Seymour	Berkeley, Michigan	1972
	Ed Muransky	Youngstown, Ohio	1981
	John Elliott	Ronkonkoma, New York	1987
Guard	Reggie McKenzie	Highland Park, Michigan	1971
	Marc Donahue	Oaklawn, Illinois	1977
	Kurt Becker	Aurora, Illinois	1981
	Stephan Humphries	Broward, Florida	1983
Center	Tom Dixon	Fort Wayne, Indiana	1983
	John Vitale	Detroit, Michigan	1988
Flanker	Jim Smith	Blue Island, Illinois	1976
	Anthony Carter	Riviera Beach, Florida	1982
Quarterback	Rick Leach	Flint, Michigan	1978
	Jim Harbaugh	Palo Alto, California	1986
Tailback	Bill Taylor	Barberton, Ohio	1971
	Rob Lytle	Fremont, Ohio	1976
	Butch Woolfolk	Westfield, New Jersey	1981
	Jamie Morris	Ayer, Massachusetts	1987
Fullback	Ed Shuttlesworth	Cincinnati, Ohio	1973
	Russell Davis	Woodbridge, Virginia	1978
Placekicker	Mike Gillette	St. Joseph, Michigan	1988
	Bob Bergeron	Fort Wayne, Indiana	1984

Note: Player listings are chronological by position with final varsity season indicated.

Michigan Football
Bo Schembechler Era - All Time Team (Defense)
1969 - 1989

Position	Name	Hometown	Year
End	Phil Seymour	Berkeley, Michigan	1970
	Mike Keller	Grand Rapids, Michigan	1971
	John Anderson	Waukesha, Wisconsin	1977
	Robert Thompson	Blue Island, Illinois	1982
Tackle	Dave Gallagher	Piqua, Ohio	1973
	Curtis Greer	Detroit, Michigan	1979
	Mike Hammerstein	Wapakoneta, Ohio	1985
	Mark Messner	Hartland, Michigan	1988
Middle Guard	Henry Hill	Detroit, Michigan	1970
	Tim Davis	Warren, Ohio	1975
Linebacker	Calvin O'Neal	Saginaw, Michigan	1976
	Ron Simpkins	Detroit, Michigan	1979
	Andy Cannavino	Cleveland, Ohio	1980
	Mike Mallory	DeKalb, Illinois	1985
Halfback	Tom Darden	Sandusky, Ohio	1971
	Randy Logan	Detroit, Michigan	1972
	Mike Jolly	Melvindale, Michigan	1979
	Brad Cochran	Royal Oak, Michigan	1985
Safety	Tom Curtis	Aurora, Ohio	1969
	Dave Brown	Akron, Ohio	1974
	Keith Bostic	Ann Arbor, Michigan	1982
	Tripp Welborne	Greensboro, N.C.	1989
Punter	Don Bracken	Thermopolis, Wyoming	1983
	Monte Robbins	Bend, Kansas	1987

Note: Player listings are chronological by position with final varsity season indicated.

ANGELIQUE S. CHENGELIS, 31, has covered the University of Michigan football team for The Detroit News since 1992. Since coming to the News from the Knoxville (Tenn.) Journal in 1990, Chengelis has also covered auto racing and University of Detroit-Mercy basketball. Chengelis was born and raised in Cincinnati, is a 1986 graduate of the University of Cincinnati and has since been working as a sportswriter. She is thankful every day for the support of her husband, David, and mother, Cleopatra Seremetis.

CHRIS MCCOSKY, 39, born and raised in Detroit, has been reporting and writing about sports since 1980. He began doing stories on the University of Michigan football program in 1983 and was the college football beat writer for the Ann Arbor News from 1988 through 1992. He presently covers the Detroit Pistons and the NBA for The Detroit News.

JOHN U. BACON, 32, was born and raised in Ann Arbor, where he attended Huron High School and the University of Michigan. He taught high school history, coached hockey and free-lanced for *The Ann Arbor Observer, Motor Trend, Bride's* and other magazines before accepting his current position at The Detroit News as a sports feature writer. He is currently finishing a book on public education.

BOB WOJNOWSKI, 34, has worked at The Detroit News since 1989. He came to the News after a six-year stint at Florida Today in Cocoa Beach. Before becoming a columnist, Wojnowski covered University of Michigan football and basketball, and a variety of other stories. Wojo is a 1983 graduate of U-M and attended high school at Battle Creek Lakeview. Wojnowski has won numerous national and state awards, and finished second in the 1994 Associated Press Sports Editors' column writing catagory.

Detroit News Sports Editor JOE FALLS became a News columnist in 1978 after more than two decades of writing sports in Detroit. His career, which began with The Associated Press in New York City, spans four decades. He was born and raised in New York and also worked for the AP in Detroit, the Detroit Times and The Detroit Free Press.

Falls, 66, has written four books, including *Daly Life: Memoirs of a World-Champion Coach*, about Detroit Pistons coach Chuck Daly. His other books dealt with former Michigan football coach Bo Schembechler, the Boston Marathon and the Detroit Tigers.

In addition, Falls has been named Michigan sportswriter of the year 11 times by the National Sportscasters and Sportswriters Association. He last won the award in 1990.